HOW TO MAKE MONEY THE JEWISH WAY

Rabbi Goldberg

RABBIGOLDBERG

How to make money the Jewish way

CHAPTER 1: THE PATH TO FINANCIAL WISDOM

In the vast tapestry of human experience, the pursuit of wealth has always been an integral thread. We embark on a journey together, not confined by cultural or religious boundaries but inspired by universal values and lessons. This book explores the timeless principles that have guided individuals, including those within the Jewish community, on their paths to financial success. Our journey begins with a realization—money, in itself, is neither inherently good nor evil. It is a tool, a means to an end, and its impact depends on the hands that wield it. Throughout history, diverse cultures have approached wealth differently, and each has left a unique imprint on the world's economic landscape.

The Jewish tradition, deeply rooted in faith and community, offers us a lens through which to examine these financial principles. At its core, the Jewish faith emphasizes the value of ethics, charity, and responsibility in financial matters. These values are not confined to one group but resonate with anyone seeking a more meaningful approach to wealth.

One of the central concepts within Judaism is "Tikkun Olam," the idea of repairing the world. This notion extends to how we handle our finances. It reminds us that our wealth should not be hoarded but used to make the world a better place. By focusing on giving back and making a positive impact, we can find deeper satisfaction in our financial success.

Throughout this book, we will delve into the stories of individuals who have embodied these principles, both within and outside the Jewish community. We'll explore their journeys, their struggles, and their triumphs. Their experiences provide valuable lessons that transcend cultural boundaries and offer insights into the human pursuit of prosperity.

As we venture through the chapters ahead, keep in mind that this is not a guide to get-rich-quick schemes. Instead, it's an exploration of enduring principles, a map to navigate the complex terrain of wealth, and a celebration of the diverse paths to financial wisdom.

In the chapters that follow, we'll explore topics such as entrepreneurship, investment strategies, philanthropy, and more. Each chapter is a piece of the puzzle, contributing to our understanding of how to make money while upholding principles that matter to us all.

So, let us embark on this journey together, learning from the wisdom of those who have walked this path before us, and weaving our own stories into the fabric of financial success. Our destination is not just financial prosperity but a richer understanding of how money can be a force for good in the world.

CHAPTER 2: THE ENTREPRENEUR'S SPIRIT

As we continue our exploration of financial wisdom, we turn our attention to the dynamic world of entrepreneurship—a realm where innovation, risk-taking, and vision converge to shape destinies. This chapter explores how the entrepreneurial spirit transcends cultural boundaries and has played a pivotal role in the financial success of many, including those within the Jewish community.

Entrepreneurship, as a concept, knows no religious or cultural limits. It's a testament to the human drive to create, innovate, and build. In every corner of the world, individuals have identified problems, envisioned solutions, and embarked on entrepreneurial journeys. This chapter, however, sheds light on how the Jewish tradition has nurtured this spirit, often leading to remarkable achievements.

One of the key principles embraced by many Jewish entrepreneurs is "Chutzpah." This Yiddish word loosely translates to audacity or nerve. It refers to the willingness to take bold risks, even in the face of uncertainty. Jewish entrepreneurs, from early pioneers to contemporary trailblazers, have often demonstrated this quality, showing that calculated audacity can be a powerful tool in wealth creation.

It's important to note that the entrepreneurial spirit doesn't guarantee success; it's a mindset and approach that involves perseverance, adaptability, and resilience. Jewish entrepreneurs have faced their share of challenges throughout history, including discrimination and adversity. Yet, their determination to overcome obstacles and pursue their dreams has been a driving force behind many successful ventures.

One notable example is the story of Levi Strauss, a German-Jewish immigrant who played a pivotal role in the development of the American frontier. His invention of durable denim jeans, initially designed for gold miners, became an iconic part of American culture. His entrepreneurial journey, like many others, underscores the power of innovation and resilience.

But entrepreneurship isn't solely about personal gain. Many Jewish entrepreneurs have also embraced the concept of "Tzedakah," which is often translated as charity but carries a deeper meaning of "justice" or "righteousness." It emphasizes the responsibility to give back to the community and support those in need. This sense of social responsibility has led to the establishment of charitable foundations and initiatives by successful Jewish entrepreneurs.

As we delve into the stories of Jewish entrepreneurs and their contributions to the business world, we see that their journeys are marked by both ambition and a commitment to making a positive impact. This fusion of personal ambition and social responsibility exemplifies how the entrepreneurial spirit can be harnessed not just for personal wealth but for the betterment of society.

CHAPTER 3: THE ART OF INVESTMENT

Our journey through the world of financial wisdom takes us to the realm of investments, where wealth is multiplied through careful allocation and strategic decisions. In this chapter, we explore the concept of investment, its significance in the pursuit of financial success, and how it intertwines with the principles often associated with the Jewish community.

Investing is a universal practice, a means by which individuals allocate their resources with the goal of generating returns over time. Whether it's investing in stocks, real estate, businesses, or other assets, the principles of sound investment apply to all, transcending cultural and religious boundaries.

Within the Jewish community, there is a long history of prudent financial management and investment. This tradition has been shaped by values such as "Tikkun Olam" and "Tzedakah," which emphasize responsible stewardship of resources and a commitment to improving the world.

One example of this commitment to responsible investment is the concept of "ethical investing" or "impact investing." Many Jewish individuals and organizations choose to invest in ventures and companies that align with their values, such as those that promote sustainability, social justice, and ethical business practices. This approach reflects a belief that financial success should not come at the expense of ethical principles.

Throughout history, Jewish individuals have also played significant roles in the world of finance and investment. The Rothschild family, for instance, established a banking dynasty in the 18th century that played a pivotal role in European finance. Their success was built on astute financial decisions and shrewd investments.

Investing wisely often involves diversification, the spreading of risk across different asset classes. Diversification is a principle embraced by investors worldwide, as it helps mitigate the impact of market volatility. Jewish investors, too, have recognized the importance of diversification in preserving and growing wealth.

As we venture deeper into the intricacies of investment, we'll explore various asset classes, investment strategies, and the mindset required for successful wealth multiplication. The journey ahead will introduce us to individuals who have harnessed the power of investment to secure their financial futures while remaining true to their principles.

This chapter is a stepping stone in our quest for financial wisdom, emphasizing the importance of making our money work for us. Investments can be a tool not only for personal gain but also for making a positive impact on the world, aligning with the values we hold dear.

CHAPTER 4: THE POWER OF NETWORKING

In the pursuit of financial wisdom, we arrive at a critical juncture—the realm of networking. While often underestimated, the connections we forge with others can profoundly impact our financial success. This chapter explores the art of networking, its universal relevance, and how it connects to the principles often associated with the Jewish community.

Networking, at its core, is about building relationships and fostering connections. It is a fundamental human activity, transcending cultural and religious boundaries. Whether in the boardrooms of Wall Street or the bustling markets of Tel Aviv, the power of connections is undeniable.

The Jewish tradition places a strong emphasis on community and interconnectedness. The concept of "Kehillah," which means community in Hebrew, highlights the importance of unity and mutual support. This sense of belonging extends to the business world, where Jewish entrepreneurs and professionals often leverage their networks to create opportunities and foster collaboration.

One example of the power of Jewish networking is the prevalence of Jewish business associations and chambers of commerce worldwide. These organizations bring together Jewish professionals and entrepreneurs to exchange ideas, share resources, and promote economic growth within their communities. Through these networks, individuals can access mentorship, funding, and valuable business connections.

In the broader context, networking is about more than just personal gain; it's a vehicle for knowledge sharing, mentorship, and community building. Successful individuals within and outside the Jewish community recognize that their achievements are often the result of the guidance and support they've received from their networks.

Networking also extends to the realm of philanthropy. Many successful Jewish individuals have used their connections to rally support for charitable causes and initiatives. By harnessing the collective power of their networks, they've been able to make a significant impact on issues ranging from education to healthcare.

As we delve deeper into the intricacies of networking, we'll explore strategies for building and nurturing meaningful connections. We'll hear the stories of individuals who have leveraged their networks to achieve financial success while upholding their principles.

This chapter serves as a reminder that wealth creation is not a solitary endeavor but a collaborative one. The bonds we form and the connections we nurture can open doors, provide guidance, and create opportunities that may have otherwise remained hidden.

CHAPTER 5: THE ART OF RESILIENCE

In the grand tapestry of financial success, one thread stands out prominently—the art of resilience. In this chapter, we delve into the concept of resilience, its universal relevance, and how it weaves into the principles often associated with the Jewish community.

Resilience is a quality that transcends cultural and religious boundaries, for it is a testament to the human spirit's ability to endure, adapt, and overcome adversity. The financial journey, like life itself, is often fraught with challenges, and resilience is the compass that guides us through the storms.

Within the Jewish tradition, the concept of "Am Yisrael Chai" echoes the enduring spirit of the Jewish people. It means "The People of Israel Live," a testament to the resilience and survival of the Jewish community throughout history, despite numerous trials and tribulations. This spirit of resilience extends to financial matters, where individuals and communities have demonstrated a remarkable ability to bounce back from setbacks and thrive.

Resilience in the face of financial adversity is a quality shared by individuals across the globe. It's the small business owner who rebuilds after a recession, the investor who remains steady during market downturns, and the worker who perseveres through tough economic times. Resilience isn't merely about weathering the storm; it's about emerging stronger on the other side.

One remarkable aspect of resilience is its connection to innovation. In times of crisis, individuals often find creative solutions to overcome challenges. Jewish inventors and entrepreneurs have a rich history of contributing groundbreaking ideas and innovations to the world. This ability to adapt and innovate in the face of adversity has played a crucial role in their financial success.

The story of Albert Einstein, a Jewish physicist who escaped Nazi Germany, serves as a powerful example of resilience and innovation. Despite facing personal and professional challenges, Einstein's work revolutionized our understanding of the universe and left an indelible mark on the world.

Resilience also intersects with the principle of "Tikkun Olam," the idea of repairing the world. Jewish individuals have channeled their resilience into philanthropic efforts, supporting causes that aim to heal and improve society. This alignment of personal strength with a commitment to making the world a better place is a testament to the enduring spirit of resilience.

As we journey further into the world of financial wisdom, we'll explore strategies for cultivating resilience, drawing inspiration from individuals who have navigated life's financial challenges with grace and determination.

This chapter reminds us that setbacks are an inevitable part of the financial journey. However, it's our resilience, the strength to persevere and adapt, that ultimately determines our success. Resilience, when combined with the principles of ethics, community, networking, and investment, becomes a powerful force in the pursuit of financial wisdom.

CHAPTER 6: THE MINDSET OF ABUNDANCE

In our exploration of financial wisdom, we now turn our attention to a fundamental aspect that shapes our approach to wealth—the mindset of abundance. This chapter delves into the concept of abundance, its universal significance, and its connection to the principles often associated with the Jewish community.

The mindset of abundance is not confined by cultural or religious boundaries; it is a perspective that transcends differences and resonates with individuals worldwide. At its core, it's about cultivating a sense of plenty, even in the face of scarcity, and recognizing that wealth extends beyond material possessions.

Within the Jewish tradition, the concept of "B'ruchah" encapsulates the idea of blessings and abundance. It's a reminder to express gratitude for the abundance we already possess in our lives, whether it's our health, relationships, or opportunities. This mindset of acknowledging and appreciating abundance aligns with the universal principle that gratitude is a powerful driver of happiness and contentment.

The mindset of abundance also extends to the belief in the limitless potential of one's own abilities and opportunities. Jewish individuals, like many others, have a rich history of pursuing education and entrepreneurship with the belief that they can achieve their goals and contribute positively to society.

One remarkable aspect of the mindset of abundance is its

connection to generosity. Those who embrace abundance are often more inclined to give back to their communities and support charitable causes. The belief that there is enough to go around encourages individuals to share their resources with others, fostering a sense of collective well-being.

The story of Julius Rosenwald, a Jewish-American businessman and philanthropist, exemplifies the mindset of abundance. As the head of Sears, Roebuck, and Company, Rosenwald used his wealth to fund the construction of thousands of schools for African-American children in the early 20th century. His legacy demonstrates that a mindset of abundance can lead to not only personal success but also significant contributions to society.

As we journey deeper into the concept of abundance, we'll explore strategies for cultivating this mindset, drawing inspiration from individuals who have harnessed the power of positivity and gratitude to navigate their financial journeys.

This chapter serves as a reminder that wealth is not merely measured by the size of one's bank account but by the richness of one's perspective. The mindset of abundance can transform how we approach financial decisions, relationships, and our overall well-being.

CHAPTER 7: THE DANCE OF RISK AND REWARD

In the intricate choreography of financial success, one cannot escape the dance of risk and reward. This chapter unravels the concept of risk and reward, its universal relevance, and its connection to the principles often associated with the Jewish community.

The dance of risk and reward knows no cultural or religious boundaries; it is a fundamental part of the human experience. It's a concept deeply rooted in the choices we make, the opportunities we seize, and the potential for both gain and loss that accompanies those choices.

Within the Jewish tradition, there is a recognition of the need to take calculated risks. The principle of "Emunah," which means faith or trust in Hebrew, encourages individuals to trust in their abilities and take bold steps toward their goals. This trust extends to their financial endeavors, where individuals often navigate the delicate balance between risk and caution.

Risk is an inherent part of the financial journey. It's the entrepreneur who invests their savings into a new venture, the investor who enters volatile markets, or the individual who pursues higher education to improve their career prospects. These actions involve varying degrees of risk, but they also hold the potential for significant rewards.

It's important to note that risk is not synonymous with recklessness. Prudent risk-taking involves careful consideration of potential outcomes and the implementation of strategies to mitigate potential downsides. This approach aligns with the universal principle of informed decision-making.

The story of George Soros, a Jewish-American investor and philanthropist, offers an illustration of risk and reward. Soros is famously known for "breaking the Bank of England" in 1992 when he bet against the British pound. His bold and strategic financial moves resulted in substantial rewards, but they were not without calculated risks.

Risk and reward are also connected to the principle of "Tzedakah." Many successful Jewish individuals recognize that their financial gains can be used to make a positive impact on society. The willingness to take financial risks is often accompanied by a commitment to give back, creating a cycle of giving and receiving. As we venture further into the world of risk and reward, we'll explore strategies for assessing and managing risk, drawing inspiration from individuals who have navigated the complex terrain of financial decisions with skill and foresight.

This chapter serves as a reminder that the path to financial success is not risk-free, but it's also not devoid of rewards. It is a journey that requires a nuanced understanding of the risks we undertake and the potential for growth and prosperity that lies on the other side.

CHAPTER 8: THE ART OF FINANCIAL PLANNING

In the grand symphony of financial wisdom, the conductor's baton of planning guides our financial endeavors. This chapter delves into the art of financial planning, its universal significance, and its connection to the principles often associated with the Jewish community.

Financial planning is a concept that transcends cultural or religious boundaries. It's a compass that helps us navigate the labyrinth of personal finance, ensuring that we chart a course towards our goals, dreams, and aspirations.

Within the Jewish tradition, there is a profound appreciation for the value of foresight and planning. The Hebrew term "Hakol L'tova" means "Everything is for the best." It reflects the belief that challenges and opportunities are part of a larger plan, and through thoughtful planning, individuals can harness these experiences to achieve their financial aspirations.

The art of financial planning is not just about budgeting or saving; it's a holistic approach that encompasses short-term and long-term goals. It's the small steps taken today that lay the foundation for a secure future. Jewish individuals often embrace this approach, recognizing the importance of preparing for life's financial twists and turns.

One remarkable aspect of financial planning is its connection to the principle of "Tzedakah." Planning involves not only securing one's financial future but also considering how to give back and make a positive impact on others. Those who engage in thoughtful financial planning often include charitable giving as an integral part of their long-term strategy.

The story of Irving Berlin, a Jewish-American composer and lyricist, serves as an example of meticulous financial planning. Despite facing hardships early in life, Berlin's careful management of his finances allowed him to build substantial wealth through his musical compositions. His legacy illustrates the rewards of foresight and planning.

Financial planning also involves a degree of risk management and investment strategy. Individuals who plan their financial futures often consider how to allocate their resources to achieve their goals. This approach aligns with the universal principle of setting priorities and making informed decisions.

As we delve deeper into the art of financial planning, we'll explore strategies for setting achievable financial goals, creating budgets, managing debt, and safeguarding our financial well-being. We'll draw inspiration from individuals who have harnessed the power of planning to transform their financial futures.

This chapter serves as a reminder that financial success is not left to chance; it is a product of deliberate choices and thoughtful strategies. Financial planning is a bridge that connects our aspirations with the realities of our financial lives.

CHAPTER 9: THE LEGACY OF PHILANTHROPY

In our journey through the landscapes of financial wisdom, we come upon a lush garden of giving—the legacy of philanthropy. This chapter explores the profound concept of philanthropy, its universal relevance, and its deep connection to the principles often associated with the Jewish community.

Philanthropy, the act of giving to support charitable causes and promote the well-being of others, is a practice that transcends cultural and religious boundaries. It's an expression of compassion and empathy, reflecting our shared humanity.

Within the Jewish tradition, philanthropy is not merely a gesture of goodwill but a fundamental principle known as "Tzedakah." This term, often translated as charity, carries a deeper meaning of "justice" or "righteousness." It emphasizes the ethical responsibility to support those in need and to promote social justice.

The legacy of philanthropy within the Jewish community is rich and varied. Jewish individuals and organizations have played pivotal roles in supporting educational institutions, healthcare facilities, cultural endeavors, and humanitarian causes. This tradition reflects the belief that wealth is not meant to be hoarded but used as a force for good.

One notable example is the story of Henry and Edsel Ford, a non-Jewish family who established the Detroit Federation of Jewish Charities (now the Jewish Federation of Metropolitan

Detroit) in the early 20th century. Their philanthropic vision extended beyond their own community, highlighting the interconnectedness of philanthropy and its potential to impact diverse groups of people.

Philanthropy is not solely about financial contributions. It also involves giving one's time, expertise, and resources to make a difference. Many Jewish individuals engage in "Tikkun Olam," the concept of repairing the world, through volunteer work and active involvement in charitable initiatives.

As we delve further into the realm of philanthropy, we'll explore the strategies for effective giving, the impact of philanthropy on individuals and communities, and the stories of those who have left lasting legacies through their acts of generosity.

This chapter serves as a reminder that wealth, when coupled with the spirit of giving, can be a catalyst for positive change. Philanthropy is a bridge that connects the fortunate with those in need, fostering a sense of compassion and shared responsibility.

CHAPTER 10: THE ART OF FINANCIAL EDUCATION

In the intricate mosaic of financial wisdom, one piece stands out prominently—the art of financial education. This chapter delves into the importance of financial education, its universal relevance, and its connection to the principles often associated with the Jewish community.

Financial education is a concept that transcends cultural and religious boundaries. It's a vital tool for individuals of all backgrounds to navigate the complexities of personal finance, make informed decisions, and secure their financial futures.

Within the Jewish tradition, there is a recognition of the value of knowledge and learning. The concept of "Chochmah," which means wisdom in Hebrew, extends to the realm of financial literacy. Jewish individuals often place a strong emphasis on educating themselves and their communities about financial matters.

Financial education encompasses a wide range of topics, including budgeting, saving, investing, debt management, and retirement planning. It's about empowering individuals with the knowledge and skills to make sound financial choices throughout their lives.

One remarkable aspect of financial education is its potential to break the cycle of financial hardship. It equips individuals with the tools to make informed decisions, avoid common pitfalls, and build a secure financial foundation for themselves and their families.

The story of Elie Wiesel, a Holocaust survivor and Nobel laureate, highlights the importance of financial education. Wiesel, in his later years, recognized the need to educate future generations about personal finance. He believed that financial education was a means to empower individuals and ensure they could make wise financial decisions.

Financial education is not solely an individual endeavor; it also involves community-wide efforts. Many Jewish organizations and institutions provide financial literacy programs and resources to support their communities in achieving financial well-being.

As we delve deeper into the art of financial education, we'll explore strategies for promoting financial literacy, the impact of education on financial decisions, and the stories of individuals who have transformed their lives through financial knowledge.

This chapter serves as a reminder that financial education is not a luxury but a necessity in today's complex financial landscape. It is a bridge that connects individuals with the information and tools they need to secure their financial futures.

In the chapters that follow, we'll continue our exploration, recognizing that each aspect of financial wisdom, whether it's ethics, community, networking, investment, resilience, the mindset of abundance, the dance of risk and reward, the art of financial planning, or the legacy of philanthropy, contributes to our holistic understanding of wealth and prosperity.

CHAPTER 11: THE ENTREPRENEURIAL SPIRIT

In our journey through the landscapes of financial wisdom, we encounter the spark of innovation and enterprise—the entrepreneurial spirit. This chapter explores the concept of entrepreneurship, its universal relevance, and its connection to the principles often associated with the Jewish community.

The entrepreneurial spirit knows no cultural or religious boundaries; it is a driving force behind innovation, economic growth, and the pursuit of dreams. It's a testament to human creativity and the desire to create something new.

Within the Jewish tradition, entrepreneurship is often embraced as a means of self-reliance and economic empowerment. The principle of "Parnassah," meaning livelihood or sustenance in Hebrew, underscores the importance of self-sufficiency. Jewish individuals have a long history of engaging in various entrepreneurial ventures, from trade and commerce to technology and finance.

Entrepreneurship is not just about starting businesses; it's about identifying opportunities, taking calculated risks, and pursuing one's passions and talents. It's about turning ideas into reality and contributing to the betterment of society.

One remarkable aspect of the entrepreneurial spirit is its potential to drive economic growth and job creation. Entrepreneurs often become the engines of prosperity, bringing new products, services, and solutions to the market. This aligns with the universal principle that innovation is a catalyst for progress.

The story of Levi Strauss, a German-Jewish immigrant to the United States, exemplifies the power of entrepreneurship. Strauss, along with his partner Jacob Davis, invented blue jeans in the 1870s. Their innovative clothing item not only became a fashion staple but also a symbol of American entrepreneurship and rugged individualism.

Entrepreneurship also intersects with the principle of "Tikkun Olam." Many Jewish entrepreneurs channel their success and resources into philanthropic endeavors, using their business acumen to address social and environmental challenges. This combination of business savvy and social responsibility reflects a holistic approach to wealth creation.

As we journey further into the world of entrepreneurship, we'll explore strategies for identifying opportunities, fostering innovation, and overcoming challenges. We'll draw inspiration from individuals who have harnessed the entrepreneurial spirit to build successful enterprises while staying true to their principles.

This chapter serves as a reminder that entrepreneurship is not limited to a select few but is a path available to those with vision, determination, and a willingness to take calculated risks. The entrepreneurial spirit is a bridge that connects ideas with action, fueling economic progress and individual empowerment.

In the chapters that follow, we'll continue our exploration, recognizing that each aspect of financial wisdom, whether it's ethics, community, networking, investment, resilience, the mindset of abundance, the dance of risk and reward, the art of financial planning, the legacy of philanthropy, or the art of financial education, contributes to our holistic understanding of wealth and prosperity.

CHAPTER 12: THE ART OF INNOVATION

In the grand tapestry of financial wisdom, we find a vibrant thread—innovation. This chapter delves into the concept of innovation, its universal relevance, and its connection to the principles often associated with the Jewish community.

Innovation is a concept that transcends cultural and religious boundaries; it is the driving force behind progress, transformation, and the betterment of human society. It's a testament to the human spirit's ability to imagine, create, and adapt.

Within the Jewish tradition, innovation is often embraced as a means of addressing challenges and driving positive change. The principle of "Chidush," meaning renewal or innovation in Hebrew, underscores the importance of adapting to evolving circumstances and finding novel solutions.

Innovation is not limited to technological breakthroughs; it extends to various aspects of life, including business, education, healthcare, and social justice. It's about thinking outside the box, challenging the status quo, and striving for continuous improvement.

One remarkable aspect of innovation is its power to disrupt and reshape industries. Innovators often identify unmet needs or inefficiencies and develop solutions that revolutionize the way we live and work. This aligns with the universal principle that progress is driven by the pursuit of betterment.

The story of Jonas Salk, an American-Jewish medical researcher, exemplifies the transformative power of innovation. In the 1950s,

Salk developed the first effective polio vaccine, a monumental achievement that saved countless lives and led to the near-eradication of the disease. His dedication to scientific innovation had a profound impact on public health.

Innovation also intersects with the principle of "Tikkun Olam." Many Jewish individuals and organizations harness the power of innovation to address pressing social and environmental challenges. They recognize that creative solutions can drive meaningful change and contribute to a more just and sustainable world.

As we venture further into the realm of innovation, we'll explore strategies for fostering creativity, embracing change, and overcoming obstacles. We'll draw inspiration from individuals who have used innovation to leave a lasting mark on their fields and society at large.

This chapter serves as a reminder that innovation is not reserved for a select few but is a mindset and a set of skills that can be cultivated by anyone. The art of innovation is a bridge that connects imagination with action, inspiring progress and shaping the future.

In the chapters that follow, we'll continue our exploration, recognizing that each aspect of financial wisdom, whether it's ethics, community, networking, investment, resilience, the mindset of abundance, the dance of risk and reward, the art of financial planning, the legacy of philanthropy, the art of financial education, or the entrepreneurial spirit, contributes to our holistic understanding of wealth and prosperity.

CHAPTER 13: THE POWER OF RESILIENCE

In our exploration of financial wisdom, we encounter a force that shapes destinies—the power of resilience. This chapter delves into the concept of resilience, its universal significance, and its connection to the principles often associated with the Jewish community.

Resilience is a quality that transcends cultural or religious boundaries; it is the ability to adapt, endure, and emerge stronger in the face of adversity. It's a testament to the human spirit's capacity to weather storms and find strength in challenging circumstances.

Within the Jewish tradition, resilience has played a pivotal role in the face of historical hardships and discrimination. The principle of "Am Yisrael Chai," which means "The People of Israel Live" in Hebrew, reflects the determination and resilience of Jewish communities in the face of challenges throughout history.

Resilience is not merely about bouncing back from setbacks; it's about using adversity as a catalyst for growth and transformation. It's the capacity to find meaning and purpose in difficult experiences and to emerge with newfound wisdom and strength.

One remarkable aspect of resilience is its power to foster innovation and creativity. Many breakthroughs and inventions have arisen from individuals who faced setbacks or failures and persevered in their pursuits. This aligns with the universal principle that resilience is a wellspring of innovation.

The story of Albert Einstein, a Jewish physicist and mathematician, exemplifies the power of resilience. Einstein faced numerous challenges and rejections early in his career, but his unwavering commitment to his scientific pursuits eventually led to groundbreaking discoveries and the development of the theory of relativity.

Resilience also intersects with the principle of "Tikkun Olam." Many Jewish individuals and organizations channel their resilience into efforts to address social and environmental challenges. They recognize that the ability to bounce back from adversity is a valuable resource for creating positive change in the world.

As we venture further into the world of resilience, we'll explore strategies for developing resilience, coping with adversity, and finding strength in difficult times. We'll draw inspiration from individuals who have harnessed the power of resilience to overcome obstacles and achieve their goals.

This chapter serves as a reminder that resilience is not a passive trait but a skill that can be cultivated and honed. The power of resilience is a bridge that connects challenges with opportunities, transforming setbacks into stepping stones toward success.

In the chapters that follow, we'll continue our exploration, recognizing that each aspect of financial wisdom, whether it's ethics, community, networking, investment, the mindset of abundance, the dance of risk and reward, the art of financial planning, the legacy of philanthropy, the art of financial education, the entrepreneurial spirit, or the art of innovation, contributes to our holistic understanding of wealth and prosperity.

CHAPTER 14: THE MINDSET OF ABUNDANCE

In our exploration of financial wisdom, we uncover a treasure—a mindset of abundance. This chapter delves into the concept of an abundance mindset, its universal relevance, and its connection to the principles often associated with the Jewish community.

An abundance mindset is a perspective that transcends cultural or religious boundaries; it is the belief that opportunities, resources, and possibilities are limitless. It's a testament to the human capacity to see abundance even in challenging circumstances.

Within the Jewish tradition, an abundance mindset is often associated with the principle of "B'ruchah," which means blessing or abundance in Hebrew. It reflects the belief that blessings and abundance can be found in all aspects of life, including financial well-being.

An abundance mindset is not about blind optimism or denial of challenges; it's about recognizing that even in times of scarcity or adversity, there are opportunities for growth, learning, and the discovery of new possibilities.

One remarkable aspect of an abundance mindset is its power to attract positive outcomes. Individuals who embrace this perspective tend to be more open to opportunities, more resilient in the face of setbacks, and more willing to take calculated risks. This aligns with the universal principle that optimism and positivity often lead to success.

The story of Henrietta Szold, a Jewish-American leader and

founder of Hadassah, exemplifies the power of an abundance mindset. Szold faced many challenges in her efforts to support Jewish healthcare and education in Palestine. Despite adversity, her unwavering belief in the potential for growth and prosperity fueled her determination and eventual success.

An abundance mindset also intersects with the principle of "Tzedakah." Many Jewish individuals who have achieved financial success recognize their responsibility to share their blessings with others. Their belief in abundance extends to the idea that wealth should be used for the betterment of the community and society as a whole.

As we delve further into the world of an abundance mindset, we'll explore strategies for cultivating positivity, embracing opportunities, and reframing challenges as stepping stones to success. We'll draw inspiration from individuals who have harnessed the power of an abundance mindset to achieve remarkable goals.

This chapter serves as a reminder that an abundance mindset is not a passive belief but a conscious choice to see the world as a place of abundance, where possibilities are endless and blessings can be found even in the most unexpected places.

In the chapters that follow, we'll continue our exploration, recognizing that each aspect of financial wisdom, whether it's ethics, community, networking, investment, resilience, the dance of risk and reward, the art of financial planning, the legacy of philanthropy, the art of financial education, the entrepreneurial spirit, the art of innovation, or the mindset of abundance, contributes to our holistic understanding of wealth and prosperity.

CHAPTER 15: THE DANCE OF RISK AND REWARD

In our voyage through the seas of financial wisdom, we come upon a captivating rhythm—the dance of risk and reward. This chapter delves into the delicate balance between risk and reward, its universal relevance, and its connection to the principles often associated with the Jewish community.

The dance of risk and reward is a concept that transcends cultural or religious boundaries; it's the fundamental interplay between the potential for gain and the possibility of loss. It's a testament to the intricate decisions we make in the pursuit of our financial goals.

Within the Jewish tradition, there is a recognition of the importance of making thoughtful and informed decisions, particularly in financial matters. The principle of "Hakarat HaTov," which means recognizing the good in Hebrew, underscores the value of gratitude and careful consideration when assessing opportunities and risks.

The dance of risk and reward is not a one-size-fits-all endeavor; it varies from person to person, depending on individual goals, risk tolerance, and time horizons. It's about finding the right tempo that aligns with your financial aspirations and values.

One remarkable aspect of the dance of risk and reward is its potential to drive innovation and progress. Risk-taking individuals and entrepreneurs often push the boundaries of what's possible, leading to breakthroughs and advancements that benefit society. This aligns with the universal principle that calculated risk is a driver of progress.

The story of George Soros, a Hungarian-Jewish-American investor and philanthropist, exemplifies the complex nature of the dance of risk and reward. Soros's bold bets in the financial markets, including famously "breaking the Bank of England," led to both great successes and notable setbacks. His career reflects the intricate decisions and calculated risks faced by investors.

The dance of risk and reward also intersects with the principle of "Tzedakah." Many Jewish individuals who have achieved financial success recognize the responsibility to use their wealth for the betterment of society. Their philanthropic efforts often involve calculated risks to address pressing social and environmental challenges.

As we explore further into the world of the dance of risk and reward, we'll delve into strategies for assessing and managing risks, making informed financial decisions, and navigating the complex landscape of investments. We'll draw inspiration from individuals who have mastered this dance to achieve their financial goals while staying true to their principles.

This chapter serves as a reminder that the dance of risk and reward is not a solo performance but a partnership between thoughtful decision-making and the pursuit of opportunities. It is a bridge that connects aspiration with action, reminding us that calculated risks can lead to fulfilling rewards.

In the chapters that follow, we'll continue our exploration, recognizing that each aspect of financial wisdom, whether it's ethics, community, networking, investment, resilience, the mindset of abundance, the art of financial planning, the legacy of philanthropy, the art of financial education, the entrepreneurial spirit, the art of innovation, or the dance of risk and reward, contributes to our holistic understanding of wealth and prosperity.

CHAPTER 16: THE ART OF FINANCIAL PLANNING

In our exploration of financial wisdom, we come upon a masterful canvas—the art of financial planning. This chapter delves into the concept of financial planning, its universal relevance, and its connection to the principles often associated with the Jewish community.

Financial planning is a concept that transcends cultural or religious boundaries; it is the strategic process of setting financial goals, making informed decisions, and creating a roadmap for achieving one's financial aspirations. It's a testament to the importance of foresight and preparedness.

Within the Jewish tradition, there is a recognition of the value of prudent financial management. The principle of "Bitachon," which means trust or confidence in Hebrew, underscores the importance of having confidence in one's financial decisions and planning for the future.

Financial planning is not a one-time task but an ongoing process that adapts to changing circumstances, goals, and life stages. It's about aligning your financial choices with your values, aspirations, and responsibilities.

One remarkable aspect of financial planning is its power to provide peace of mind and a sense of control over one's financial destiny. It empowers individuals to make informed decisions, set realistic goals, and navigate financial challenges with confidence. This aligns with the universal principle that preparation is a key to success.

The story of Sir Moses Montefiore, a British-Jewish philanthropist and financier, exemplifies the importance of financial planning. Montefiore's meticulous financial management allowed him to support numerous charitable causes throughout his life, leaving a lasting legacy of philanthropy. His financial planning skills enabled him to make a significant impact on society.

Financial planning also intersects with the principle of "Tzedakah." Many Jewish individuals who engage in financial planning view it as a means of ensuring they have the resources to support charitable endeavors and promote social justice. It reflects a holistic approach to wealth management.

As we venture further into the world of financial planning, we'll explore strategies for setting financial goals, budgeting, saving, investing, retirement planning, and estate planning. We'll draw inspiration from individuals who have used the art of financial planning to secure their financial futures and make a positive impact on the world.

This chapter serves as a reminder that financial planning is not a luxury but a critical tool for achieving financial security and realizing one's dreams. The art of financial planning is a bridge that connects financial goals with actionable strategies, allowing individuals to shape their financial destinies.

CHAPTER 17: THE LEGACY OF PHILANTHROPY

In our journey through the realms of financial wisdom, we arrive at a place of profound significance—the legacy of philanthropy. This chapter explores the concept of philanthropy, its universal relevance, and its connection to the principles often associated with the Jewish community.

Philanthropy is a concept that transcends cultural or religious boundaries; it is the act of giving, whether through time, resources, or expertise, to benefit others and promote the well-being of society. It's a testament to the compassion and empathy inherent in humanity.

Within the Jewish tradition, philanthropy is deeply rooted in the principle of "Tzedakah," which means charity or righteousness in Hebrew. It reflects the belief that individuals have a moral responsibility to give back to their communities and support those in need.

Philanthropy is not limited to financial donations; it encompasses a wide range of acts of kindness, including volunteering, mentorship, and advocacy. It's about making a positive impact on the lives of others and leaving a legacy of compassion and generosity.

One remarkable aspect of philanthropy is its potential to create lasting change and inspire others to do the same. Philanthropic individuals and organizations often catalyze social movements, address pressing issues, and build stronger, more resilient communities. This aligns with the universal principle that collective action can drive positive transformation.

The story of Julius Rosenwald, a Jewish-American businessman and philanthropist, exemplifies the power of philanthropy to uplift communities. Rosenwald's collaboration with Booker T. Washington led to the establishment of Rosenwald Schools, which provided education to African American children in the segregated South. His philanthropic legacy continues to impact generations.

Philanthropy also intersects with the principle of "Tikkun Olam." Many Jewish individuals and organizations engage in philanthropic efforts as a means of repairing and healing the world. They recognize that by giving back, they can contribute to a more just and compassionate society.

As we delve further into the world of philanthropy, we'll explore strategies for effective giving, the impact of philanthropy on personal fulfillment, and the role of philanthropy in addressing global challenges. We'll draw inspiration from individuals who have left enduring legacies of kindness and generosity.

This chapter serves as a reminder that philanthropy is not an exclusive privilege but a fundamental aspect of the human experience. The legacy of philanthropy is a bridge that connects individuals with the broader community, fostering a sense of unity and shared responsibility.

In the chapters that follow, we'll continue our exploration, recognizing that each aspect of financial wisdom, whether it's ethics, community, networking, investment, resilience, the mindset of abundance, the dance of risk and reward, the art of financial planning, the art of financial education, the entrepreneurial spirit, the art of innovation, or the legacy of philanthropy, contributes to our holistic understanding of wealth and prosperity.

CHAPTER 18: THE ART OF FINANCIAL EDUCATION

In our exploration of financial wisdom, we arrive at a vital crossroads—the art of financial education. This chapter delves into the concept of financial education, its universal relevance, and its connection to the principles often associated with the Jewish community.

Financial education is a concept that transcends cultural or religious boundaries; it is the process of acquiring knowledge and skills related to personal finance, investing, and money management. It's a testament to the importance of informed decision-making in the realm of finances.

Within the Jewish tradition, there is a recognition of the value of financial literacy. The principle of "Chachmah," which means wisdom in Hebrew, underscores the importance of acquiring knowledge and making wise choices, particularly in matters of money.

Financial education is not merely about numbers and calculations; it encompasses a holistic understanding of financial well-being. It's about making informed choices that align with one's values, goals, and aspirations.

One remarkable aspect of financial education is its potential to empower individuals to take control of their financial destinies. It equips them with the tools to make informed decisions, set realistic goals, and navigate the complex financial landscape. This aligns with the universal principle that knowledge is a source of empowerment.

The story of Elie Wiesel, a Jewish-American writer, professor, and Nobel laureate, exemplifies the importance of education and financial literacy. Wiesel's experience as a Holocaust survivor led him to advocate for education and awareness about the Holocaust. His work underscored the profound impact of knowledge in shaping our understanding of history and its implications.

Financial education also intersects with the principle of "Tzedakah." Many Jewish individuals and organizations recognize that financial education is a means of promoting economic self-sufficiency and reducing inequalities. They view it as a way to empower individuals and communities to achieve financial security.

As we delve further into the world of financial education, we'll explore strategies for acquiring financial literacy, resources for expanding financial knowledge, and the role of education in promoting economic well-being. We'll draw inspiration from individuals and organizations that have made significant strides in advancing financial education.

This chapter serves as a reminder that financial education is not a luxury but a fundamental skill that can improve the quality of life and promote financial independence. The art of financial education is a bridge that connects knowledge with action, enabling individuals to make informed and empowered financial decisions.

In the chapters that follow, we'll continue our exploration, recognizing that each aspect of financial wisdom, whether it's ethics, community, networking, investment, resilience, the mindset of abundance, the dance of risk and reward, the art of financial planning, the legacy of philanthropy, the art of financial education, the entrepreneurial spirit, the art of innovation, or the legacy of wisdom, contributes to our holistic understanding of wealth and prosperity.

CHAPTER 19: THE ENTREPRENEURIAL SPIRIT

In our expedition through the landscape of financial wisdom, we encounter a fiery spirit—the entrepreneurial spirit. This chapter explores the concept of entrepreneurship, its universal relevance, and its connection to the principles often associated with the Jewish community.

The entrepreneurial spirit is a concept that transcends cultural or religious boundaries; it is the drive, creativity, and determination to identify opportunities, take calculated risks, and create new ventures. It's a testament to the human capacity for innovation and enterprise.

Within the Jewish tradition, there is a recognition of the value of entrepreneurship. The principle of "Hiddur Mitzvah," which means enhancing the performance of a commandment in Hebrew, underscores the importance of going above and beyond in one's pursuits. It reflects the idea that entrepreneurship is a means of enhancing one's contributions to society.

The entrepreneurial spirit is not limited to starting businesses; it encompasses a mindset of problem-solving, resilience, and adaptability. It's about seeing challenges as opportunities and pursuing goals with determination.

One remarkable aspect of the entrepreneurial spirit is its potential to drive economic growth, create jobs, and spur innovation. Entrepreneurs often lead the way in developing new technologies, products, and services that benefit society. This aligns with the universal principle that innovation is a catalyst for progress.

The story of Estée Lauder, a Jewish-American entrepreneur and cosmetics mogul, exemplifies the power of the entrepreneurial spirit. Lauder's journey from mixing skincare products in her kitchen to building a global beauty empire demonstrates the transformative potential of entrepreneurship. Her legacy continues to shape the beauty industry.

The entrepreneurial spirit also intersects with the principle of "Tzedakah." Many Jewish entrepreneurs view their success as an opportunity to give back to their communities and support charitable causes. They recognize that entrepreneurship can be a force for positive change in society.

As we venture further into the world of the entrepreneurial spirit, we'll explore strategies for fostering innovation, overcoming challenges, and cultivating an entrepreneurial mindset. We'll draw inspiration from individuals who have harnessed the power of entrepreneurship to achieve remarkable goals.

This chapter serves as a reminder that the entrepreneurial spirit is not confined to a select few but is a quality that can be cultivated and embraced by individuals from all walks of life. It is a bridge that connects aspiration with action, inspiring individuals to pursue their dreams and make a lasting impact.

In the chapters that follow, we'll continue our exploration, recognizing that each aspect of financial wisdom, whether it's ethics, community, networking, investment, resilience, the mindset of abundance, the dance of risk and reward, the art of financial planning, the legacy of philanthropy, the art of financial education, the entrepreneurial spirit, the art of innovation, or the legacy of wisdom, contributes to our holistic understanding of wealth and prosperity.

CHAPTER 20: THE ART OF INNOVATION

In our odyssey through the world of financial wisdom, we stumble upon a spark of brilliance—the art of innovation. This chapter explores the concept of innovation, its universal relevance, and its connection to the principles often associated with the Jewish community.

Innovation is a concept that transcends cultural or religious boundaries; it is the process of creating and implementing new ideas, products, or solutions that bring about positive change. It's a testament to human ingenuity and the pursuit of progress.

Within the Jewish tradition, there is a recognition of the value of innovation. The principle of "Chidush," which means renewal or innovation in Hebrew, underscores the importance of continually seeking new ways to improve and enrich life. It reflects the idea that innovation is a means of advancing society.

Innovation is not limited to groundbreaking inventions; it encompasses a mindset of curiosity, adaptability, and problem-solving. It's about approaching challenges with a fresh perspective and finding creative solutions.

One remarkable aspect of innovation is its potential to transform industries, enhance efficiency, and improve quality of life. Innovators often lead the way in addressing complex global challenges, from healthcare to environmental sustainability. This aligns with the universal principle that progress is driven by those willing to question the status quo.

The story of Albert Einstein, a Jewish physicist renowned for his theory of relativity, exemplifies the power of innovation. Einstein's groundbreaking ideas revolutionized our understanding of the universe and had a profound impact on scientific progress. His legacy continues to inspire scientists and innovators worldwide.

Innovation also intersects with the principle of "Tikkun Olam." Many Jewish individuals and organizations engage in innovative efforts aimed at repairing and improving the world. They recognize that innovation can be a force for positive change and social justice.

As we delve further into the world of innovation, we'll explore strategies for fostering creativity, embracing change, and cultivating an innovative mindset. We'll draw inspiration from individuals and organizations that have harnessed the power of innovation to address pressing global issues.

This chapter serves as a reminder that innovation is not reserved for a select few but is a quality that can be nurtured and cultivated by individuals from all backgrounds. It is a bridge that connects imagination with impact, inspiring individuals to envision a better future and work towards its realization.

In the chapters that follow, we'll continue our exploration, recognizing that each aspect of financial wisdom, whether it's ethics, community, networking, investment, resilience, the mindset of abundance, the dance of risk and reward, the art of financial planning, the legacy of philanthropy, the art of financial education, the entrepreneurial spirit, the art of innovation, or the legacy of wisdom, contributes to our holistic understanding of wealth and prosperity.

CHAPTER 21: THE LEGACY OF WISDOM

In our voyage through the realm of financial wisdom, we arrive at a treasure trove—the legacy of wisdom. This chapter explores the enduring value of wisdom, its universal relevance, and its connection to the principles often associated with the Jewish community.

Wisdom is a concept that transcends cultural or religious boundaries; it is the accumulation of knowledge, experience, and insights that guide thoughtful decision-making and virtuous living. It's a testament to the timeless pursuit of understanding life's complexities.

Within the Jewish tradition, there is a profound reverence for wisdom. The principle of "Chochmah," which means wisdom in Hebrew, underscores the importance of seeking knowledge, making informed choices, and living a life of purpose and integrity.

Wisdom is not merely about the accumulation of facts or information; it encompasses a deep understanding of the human condition and the ability to apply that understanding to navigate life's challenges. It's about making choices that reflect one's values and contribute to the betterment of society.

One remarkable aspect of wisdom is its capacity to inspire and guide future generations. Wisdom is often passed down through stories, teachings, and ethical principles, shaping the moral compass of individuals and societies. This aligns with the universal principle that the pursuit of wisdom is a timeless endeavor.

The story of Rabbi Hillel the Elder, a revered Jewish sage from antiquity, exemplifies the enduring impact of wisdom. Hillel's teachings on ethics, humility, and compassion continue to inspire individuals seeking to live virtuous lives. His legacy serves as a testament to the enduring value of wisdom.

Wisdom also intersects with the principle of "Tzedakah." Many Jewish individuals and organizations view wisdom as a means of promoting social justice and ethical conduct. They recognize that wisdom is a guide for making just and compassionate decisions.

As we venture further into the world of wisdom, we'll explore the ways in which wisdom is acquired, the role of mentors and role models, and the impact of wisdom on ethical decision-making. We'll draw inspiration from individuals who have left behind legacies of wisdom that continue to shape our world.

This chapter serves as a reminder that wisdom is not a relic of the past but a living, breathing force that can guide individuals in their pursuit of meaningful and ethical lives. The legacy of wisdom is a bridge that connects the past with the present, reminding us of the enduring value of timeless principles.

In the chapters that follow, we'll continue our exploration, recognizing that each aspect of financial wisdom, whether it's ethics, community, networking, investment, resilience, the mindset of abundance, the dance of risk and reward, the art of financial planning, the legacy of philanthropy, the art of financial education, the entrepreneurial spirit, the art of innovation, or the legacy of wisdom, contributes to our holistic understanding of wealth and prosperity.

CHAPTER 22: THE ART OF ADAPTATION

In our exploration of financial wisdom, we come across a crucial skill—the art of adaptation. This chapter delves into the concept of adaptation, its universal relevance, and its connection to the principles often associated with the Jewish community.

Adaptation is a concept that transcends cultural or religious boundaries; it is the ability to adjust to changing circumstances, embrace innovation, and thrive in the face of uncertainty. It's a testament to human resilience and the capacity for growth.

Within the Jewish tradition, there is a recognition of the value of adaptation. The principle of "Yisrael," which means to wrestle with God in Hebrew, underscores the importance of facing challenges with determination and adaptability. It reflects the idea that adaptation is a means of overcoming obstacles and growing stronger.

Adaptation is not merely about reacting to change; it encompasses a proactive mindset of flexibility, creativity, and perseverance. It's about viewing change as an opportunity for growth and transformation.

One remarkable aspect of adaptation is its potential to lead to innovation and progress. Individuals and communities that embrace change often find new ways of doing things, discover hidden strengths, and navigate uncharted territory. This aligns with the universal principle that adaptability is a source of resilience.

The story of the Jewish diaspora, a historical example of adaptation, exemplifies the power of resilience and innovation in the face of adversity. Throughout history, Jewish communities have faced dispersion and persecution but have adapted and thrived in new environments. Their resilience and ability to preserve their cultural identity serve as an inspiration to many.

Adaptation also intersects with the principle of "Tikkun Olam." Many Jewish individuals and organizations engage in adaptive efforts aimed at repairing and improving the world. They recognize that adaptation is a means of addressing pressing global challenges and fostering a more just and sustainable future.

As we delve further into the world of adaptation, we'll explore strategies for developing adaptability, embracing change, and navigating uncertainty with confidence. We'll draw inspiration from individuals and organizations that have harnessed the power of adaptation to overcome significant challenges.

This chapter serves as a reminder that adaptation is not a sign of weakness but a mark of resilience and growth. The art of adaptation is a bridge that connects challenges with opportunities, inspiring individuals to embrace change as a path to progress.

In the chapters that follow, we'll continue our exploration, recognizing that each aspect of financial wisdom, whether it's ethics, community, networking, investment, resilience, the mindset of abundance, the dance of risk and reward, the art of financial planning, the legacy of philanthropy, the art of financial education, the entrepreneurial spirit, the art of innovation, the legacy of wisdom, or the art of adaptation, contributes to our holistic understanding of wealth and prosperity.

CHAPTER 23: THE POWER OF RESILIENCE

As we continue our journey through the landscape of financial wisdom, we encounter an indispensable quality—the power of resilience. This chapter explores the concept of resilience, its universal relevance, and its connection to the principles often associated with the Jewish community.

Resilience is a concept that transcends cultural or religious boundaries; it is the capacity to withstand adversity, recover from setbacks, and emerge stronger from challenges. It's a testament to the human spirit's ability to endure and thrive.

Within the Jewish tradition, there is a profound recognition of the value of resilience. The principle of "Am Yisrael Chai," which means the people of Israel live in Hebrew, underscores the enduring nature of the Jewish community despite historical hardships. It reflects the idea that resilience is a means of preserving identity and heritage.

Resilience is not merely about bouncing back from difficulties; it encompasses a mindset of determination, adaptability, and hope. It's about facing adversity with courage and finding strength in the face of uncertainty.

One remarkable aspect of resilience is its potential to inspire and uplift. Resilient individuals and communities often serve as beacons of hope, demonstrating that even in the darkest of times, the human spirit can endure and triumph. This aligns with the universal principle that resilience is a source of inspiration.

The story of Anne Frank, a young Jewish girl who documented her life in hiding during the Holocaust, exemplifies the power of resilience. Despite the unimaginable hardships she faced, Anne's words have continued to inspire generations with their message of hope and resilience.

Resilience also intersects with the principle of "Tikkun Olam." Many Jewish individuals and organizations engage in resilient efforts aimed at repairing and healing the world. They recognize that resilience is a means of overcoming societal challenges and working towards a better future.

As we delve deeper into the world of resilience, we'll explore strategies for developing resilience, fostering hope, and navigating adversity with grace. We'll draw inspiration from individuals and communities that have harnessed the power of resilience to overcome formidable obstacles.

This chapter serves as a reminder that resilience is not a rare quality but a strength that lies within each of us. The power of resilience is a bridge that connects trials with triumphs, inspiring individuals to face challenges with courage and emerge from them with newfound strength.

In the chapters that follow, we'll continue our exploration, recognizing that each aspect of financial wisdom, whether it's ethics, community, networking, investment, the mindset of abundance, the dance of risk and reward, the art of financial planning, the legacy of philanthropy, the art of financial education, the entrepreneurial spirit, the art of innovation, the legacy of wisdom, the art of adaptation, or the power of resilience, contributes to our holistic understanding of wealth and prosperity.

CHAPTER 24: THE DANCE OF RISK AND REWARD

As we continue our exploration of financial wisdom, we find ourselves on a tightrope—the dance of risk and reward. This chapter delves into the delicate balance between risk and reward, its universal relevance, and its connection to the principles often associated with the Jewish community.

The dance of risk and reward is a concept that transcends cultural or religious boundaries; it is the intricate choreography of making decisions that involve varying degrees of uncertainty and potential gain. It's a testament to the human capacity for calculated judgment.

Within the Jewish tradition, there is a profound recognition of the value of managing risk and understanding the potential rewards. The principle of "Hochachah," which means wisdom in judgment in Hebrew, underscores the importance of making thoughtful choices in financial matters. It reflects the idea that the dance of risk and reward requires careful consideration.

The dance of risk and reward is not merely about taking reckless chances or avoiding all risks; it encompasses a mindset of prudence, assessment, and strategic thinking. It's about recognizing that every financial decision involves an element of risk and being prepared to manage that risk effectively.

One remarkable aspect of the dance of risk and reward is its potential to lead to growth and prosperity. Individuals and organizations that skillfully navigate this dance often find opportunities for innovation, growth, and financial success. This aligns with the universal principle that calculated risk-taking is a driver of progress.

The story of Warren Buffett, one of the world's most successful investors, exemplifies the art of the dance of risk and reward. Buffett's disciplined approach to investing involves carefully assessing risks and making long-term investments in companies with strong fundamentals. His investment philosophy has yielded significant rewards over the years.

The dance of risk and reward also intersects with the principle of "Tzedakah." Many Jewish individuals and organizations recognize that effectively managing risk can lead to greater resources for charitable giving and philanthropic efforts. They understand that responsible risk-taking can benefit not only themselves but also society at large.

As we waltz further into the world of the dance of risk and reward, we'll explore strategies for assessing risk, making informed decisions, and balancing the pursuit of rewards with prudent caution. We'll draw inspiration from individuals and organizations that have mastered this dance to achieve financial success.

This chapter serves as a reminder that the dance of risk and reward is not a gamble but a carefully choreographed performance that requires skill, insight, and wisdom. It is a dance that connects opportunity with responsibility, inspiring individuals to make financial decisions that align with their values and goals.

In the chapters that follow, we'll continue our exploration, recognizing that each aspect of financial wisdom, whether it's ethics, community, networking, investment, the mindset of abundance, the art of financial planning, the legacy of philanthropy, the art of financial education, the entrepreneurial spirit, the art of innovation, the legacy of wisdom, the art of adaptation, the power of resilience, or the dance of risk and reward, contributes to our holistic understanding of wealth and prosperity.

CHAPTER 25: THE ART OF FINANCIAL PLANNING

In our journey through the realm of financial wisdom, we arrive at a crucial juncture—the art of financial planning. This chapter delves into the significance of financial planning, its universal relevance, and its connection to the principles often associated with the Jewish community.

Financial planning is a concept that transcends cultural or religious boundaries; it is the process of setting financial goals, creating a roadmap to achieve them, and ensuring financial well-being. It's a testament to the importance of thoughtful preparation.

Within the Jewish tradition, there is a profound recognition of the value of planning for the future. The principle of "Hachlata," which means resolution or determination in Hebrew, underscores the importance of setting clear financial goals and taking determined steps to achieve them. It reflects the idea that financial planning requires foresight and intention.

Financial planning is not merely about budgeting or saving; it encompasses a holistic approach to managing one's financial life. It's about aligning one's financial decisions with their values, goals, and long-term aspirations. It's a proactive stance towards financial well-being.

One remarkable aspect of financial planning is its potential to provide security and peace of mind. Individuals and families that engage in thorough financial planning often experience greater financial stability and a reduced sense of financial stress. This aligns with the universal principle that planning is a source of security.

The story of the Rothschild family, known for their financial acumen and careful planning, exemplifies the art of financial planning. The Rothschilds established one of the most successful banking dynasties in history through meticulous financial planning and strategic decision-making. Their legacy serves as a testament to the power of thoughtful preparation.

Financial planning also intersects with the principle of "Tzedakah." Many Jewish individuals and organizations recognize that effective financial planning can lead to greater resources for charitable giving and philanthropy. They understand that responsible financial management can benefit not only themselves but also those in need.

As we delve deeper into the art of financial planning, we'll explore strategies for setting financial goals, creating budgets, managing debt, saving for retirement, and building wealth. We'll draw inspiration from individuals and organizations that have harnessed the power of financial planning to achieve their dreams.

This chapter serves as a reminder that financial planning is not a luxury but a necessary skill for navigating life's financial challenges. The art of financial planning is a bridge that connects dreams with reality, inspiring individuals to take control of their financial destinies.

CHAPTER 26: THE LEGACY OF PHILANTHROPY

In our ongoing exploration of financial wisdom, we arrive at a chapter dedicated to the legacy of philanthropy. This chapter delves into the significance of philanthropy, its universal relevance, and its connection to the principles often associated with the Jewish community.

Philanthropy is a concept that transcends cultural or religious boundaries; it is the act of giving back, contributing to the well-being of others, and making a positive impact on society. It's a testament to the capacity for generosity and empathy that resides within each of us.

Within the Jewish tradition, there is a profound recognition of the value of giving to those in need. The principle of "Tzedakah," often translated as charity, underscores the importance of justice and righteousness in philanthropic endeavors. It reflects the idea that philanthropy is a means of creating a more equitable and compassionate world.

Philanthropy is not merely about writing a check or making a donation; it encompasses a broader commitment to making a difference. It's about recognizing that wealth carries with it a responsibility to support causes and organizations that align with one's values and priorities. It's an expression of social consciousness and ethical commitment.

One remarkable aspect of philanthropy is its potential to inspire positive change. Individuals and organizations that engage in philanthropic efforts often catalyze progress in areas such as education, healthcare, social justice, and the arts. This aligns with the universal principle that philanthropy is a source of transformation.

The story of Andrew Carnegie, a Scottish-American industrialist and philanthropist, exemplifies the legacy of philanthropy. Carnegie amassed great wealth through his steel business and then dedicated much of his fortune to building libraries, schools, and cultural institutions. His legacy continues to enrich communities across the world.

Philanthropy also intersects with the principle of "Tikkun Olam." Many Jewish individuals and organizations recognize that philanthropic acts are a means of repairing and healing the world. They understand that giving back is a way of fulfilling the moral imperative to make the world a better place for all.

As we delve deeper into the legacy of philanthropy, we'll explore strategies for effective giving, the impact of philanthropy on individuals and society, and the role of philanthropy in creating lasting change. We'll draw inspiration from individuals and organizations that have left a significant philanthropic mark on the world.

This chapter serves as a reminder that philanthropy is not the privilege of the wealthy but a powerful force that can be harnessed by individuals and communities to address pressing societal challenges. The legacy of philanthropy is a bridge that connects prosperity with purpose, inspiring individuals to leave a positive mark on the world.

CHAPTER 27: THE ART OF FINANCIAL EDUCATION

In our continuous exploration of financial wisdom, we arrive at the chapter dedicated to the art of financial education. This chapter delves into the significance of financial education, its universal relevance, and its connection to the principles often associated with the Jewish community.

Financial education is a concept that transcends cultural or religious boundaries; it is the process of acquiring knowledge and skills related to managing personal finances, investments, and economic principles. It's a testament to the importance of informed decision-making.

Within the Jewish tradition, there is a profound recognition of the value of knowledge and education. The principle of "Chinuch," which means education in Hebrew, underscores the importance of continuous learning and intellectual growth. It reflects the idea that financial education is a means of empowerment.

Financial education is not merely about understanding numbers and budgets; it encompasses a broader commitment to financial literacy and competency. It's about recognizing that a lack of financial knowledge can lead to poor decision-making and financial vulnerability. It's an investment in one's own future.

One remarkable aspect of financial education is its potential to level the playing field. Individuals and communities that prioritize financial education often empower themselves to make informed financial choices, escape cycles of debt, and build wealth. This aligns with the universal principle that education is a path to equality.

The story of Suze Orman, a renowned financial expert and educator, exemplifies the art of financial education. Orman's journey from a waitress to a highly influential financial educator demonstrates the transformative power of financial knowledge. Her books, television shows, and speeches have empowered millions to take control of their finances.

Financial education also intersects with the principle of "Talmud Torah." Many Jewish individuals and organizations recognize that financial literacy is a form of learning and growth. They understand that education is not limited to the classroom but extends to all aspects of life, including finances.

As we delve deeper into the art of financial education, we'll explore strategies for acquiring financial knowledge, the impact of financial education on individuals and communities, and the role of education in promoting financial well-being. We'll draw inspiration from individuals and organizations that have made financial education their mission.

This chapter serves as a reminder that financial education is not a luxury but a necessity in today's complex financial landscape. The art of financial education is a torch that illuminates the path to financial security and independence, inspiring individuals to take charge of their financial destinies.

CHAPTER 28: THE ENTREPRENEURIAL SPIRIT

In our journey through the realm of financial wisdom, we arrive at a chapter dedicated to the entrepreneurial spirit. This chapter delves into the significance of entrepreneurship, its universal relevance, and its connection to the principles often associated with the Jewish community.

The entrepreneurial spirit is a concept that transcends cultural or religious boundaries; it is the drive, creativity, and ambition to create new ventures, innovate, and take calculated risks in the pursuit of economic success. It's a testament to the human capacity for innovation and enterprise.

Within the Jewish tradition, there is a profound recognition of the value of enterprise and creativity. The principle of "Yezter HaRa," which means the evil inclination in Hebrew, underscores the idea that ambition and desire, when harnessed constructively, can lead to remarkable achievements. It reflects the notion that entrepreneurship is a means of fulfilling one's potential.

The entrepreneurial spirit is not merely about starting a business; it encompasses a broader commitment to innovation, problem-solving, and adaptability. It's about recognizing that entrepreneurship is a driver of economic growth, job creation, and societal progress. It's a catalyst for change.

One remarkable aspect of the entrepreneurial spirit is its potential to transform industries and economies. Entrepreneurs and innovators often disrupt established norms, create new markets, and drive technological advancements. This aligns with the universal principle that innovation is a force of progress.

The story of Steve Jobs, the co-founder of Apple Inc., exemplifies the entrepreneurial spirit. Jobs' relentless pursuit of innovation and his commitment to creating beautifully designed products revolutionized the technology industry. His legacy continues to inspire entrepreneurs worldwide.

The entrepreneurial spirit also intersects with the principle of "Pikuach Nefesh." Many Jewish individuals and organizations recognize that entrepreneurship can address pressing societal challenges, create jobs, and improve lives. They understand that entrepreneurship is not just about profit but also about social impact.

As we delve deeper into the entrepreneurial spirit, we'll explore the qualities and mindset of successful entrepreneurs, the challenges they face, and the role of entrepreneurship in economic development. We'll draw inspiration from individuals and organizations that have embraced the entrepreneurial spirit to bring about positive change.

This chapter serves as a reminder that the entrepreneurial spirit is not limited to a select few but is a trait that can be nurtured and cultivated by individuals from all walks of life. The entrepreneurial spirit is a beacon that guides innovators to forge new paths, inspire change, and shape the future.

In the chapters that follow, we'll continue our exploration, recognizing that each aspect of financial wisdom, whether it's ethics, community, networking, investment, the mindset of abundance, the dance of risk and reward, the art of financial planning, the legacy of philanthropy, the art of financial education, the entrepreneurial spirit, the art of innovation, the legacy of wisdom, the art of adaptation, the power of resilience, or the entrepreneurial spirit, contributes to our holistic understanding of wealth and prosperity.

CHAPTER 29: THE ART OF INNOVATION

In our exploration of financial wisdom, we now venture into a chapter dedicated to the art of innovation. This chapter delves into the significance of innovation, its universal relevance, and its connection to the principles often associated with the Jewish community.

Innovation is a concept that transcends cultural or religious boundaries; it is the process of introducing novel ideas, products, or methods that bring about positive change and progress. It's a testament to human creativity and adaptability.

Within the Jewish tradition, there is a profound recognition of the value of innovation. The principle of "Hiddush," which means renewal in Hebrew, underscores the idea that innovation is essential for personal and societal growth. It reflects the notion that innovation is a means of improving lives.

Innovation is not merely about groundbreaking inventions; it encompasses a broader commitment to continuous improvement, problem-solving, and creative thinking. It's about recognizing that innovation can occur in all aspects of life, from technology to culture to business. It's a catalyst for evolution.

One remarkable aspect of innovation is its potential to transform industries and societies. Innovations in science, technology, and the arts often lead to profound shifts in how we live, work, and interact. This aligns with the universal principle that innovation drives progress.

The story of Albert Einstein, the renowned physicist, exemplifies the art of innovation. Einstein's groundbreaking theories of relativity revolutionized our understanding of the universe. His innovative thinking and relentless pursuit of knowledge continue to inspire scientists and thinkers worldwide.

Innovation also intersects with the principle of "Chidush HaTeva." Many Jewish individuals and organizations recognize that innovation can address pressing societal challenges, enhance efficiency, and improve the quality of life. They understand that innovation is not just about novelty but also about practicality.

As we delve deeper into the art of innovation, we'll explore the creative process, the mindset of innovators, and the impact of innovation on individuals and societies. We'll draw inspiration from individuals and organizations that have embraced innovation to bring about positive change.

This chapter serves as a reminder that innovation is not the exclusive domain of geniuses but is a mindset and a process that can be cultivated by individuals and communities. The art of innovation is a guiding light that encourages us to question the status quo, seek improvements, and envision a better future.

In the chapters that follow, we'll continue our exploration, recognizing that each aspect of financial wisdom, whether it's ethics, community, networking, investment, the mindset of abundance, the dance of risk and reward, the art of financial planning, the legacy of philanthropy, the art of financial education, the entrepreneurial spirit, the art of innovation, the legacy of wisdom, the art of adaptation, the power of resilience, or the art of innovation, contributes to our holistic understanding of wealth and prosperity.

CHAPTER 30: THE LEGACY OF WISDOM

In our journey through the realms of financial wisdom, we arrive at a chapter dedicated to the legacy of wisdom. This chapter delves into the significance of wisdom, its universal relevance, and its connection to the principles often associated with the Jewish community.

Wisdom is a concept that transcends cultural or religious boundaries; it is the accumulation of knowledge, experience, and insight over time. Wisdom reflects the depth of human understanding and the ability to make sound decisions based on discernment.

Within the Jewish tradition, there is a profound reverence for wisdom. The principle of "Chochmah," which means wisdom in Hebrew, underscores the idea that wisdom is a precious treasure. It reflects the notion that wisdom is a means of navigating life's challenges and making ethical choices.

Wisdom is not merely about knowing facts or possessing information; it encompasses a broader commitment to moral values, empathy, and the ability to discern right from wrong. It's about recognizing that wisdom is not static but evolves with each generation. It's a compass for ethical living.

One remarkable aspect of wisdom is its potential to guide individuals and societies through complex moral dilemmas and ethical decisions. Wise leaders and thinkers often provide insights that illuminate the path toward justice, compassion, and human flourishing. This aligns with the universal principle that wisdom is a beacon of light in the darkness of uncertainty.

The story of King Solomon, a figure revered in Jewish tradition, exemplifies the legacy of wisdom. Solomon's renowned wisdom is celebrated in literature and folklore. His ability to discern truth and render just decisions continues to inspire leaders and seekers of wisdom.

Wisdom also intersects with the principle of "Da'as Torah." Many Jewish individuals and organizations recognize the importance of seeking guidance from wise mentors and leaders. They understand that wisdom is not solely an individual pursuit but a collective endeavor.

As we delve deeper into the legacy of wisdom, we'll explore the qualities of wise individuals, the cultivation of wisdom, and the role of wisdom in ethical decision-making. We'll draw inspiration from individuals and organizations that have embraced the legacy of wisdom to foster harmony and justice.

This chapter serves as a reminder that wisdom is not confined to the elderly but is a virtue that can be cultivated by individuals of all ages. The legacy of wisdom is a guiding star that encourages us to seek knowledge, show empathy, and make choices that honor our shared humanity.

In the chapters that follow, we'll continue our exploration, recognizing that each aspect of financial wisdom, whether it's ethics, community, networking, investment, the mindset of abundance, the dance of risk and reward, the art of financial planning, the legacy of philanthropy, the art of financial education, the entrepreneurial spirit, the art of innovation, the legacy of wisdom, the art of adaptation, the power of resilience, or the legacy of wisdom, contributes to our holistic understanding of wealth and prosperity.

CHAPTER 31: THE ART OF ADAPTATION

In our exploration of financial wisdom, we now venture into a chapter dedicated to the art of adaptation. This chapter delves into the significance of adaptation, its universal relevance, and its connection to the principles often associated with the Jewish community.

Adaptation is a concept that transcends cultural or religious boundaries; it is the ability to adjust to changing circumstances and environments. It's the recognition that change is a constant in life, and the capacity to respond effectively is a valuable skill.

Within the Jewish tradition, there is a profound appreciation for the art of adaptation. The principle of "Shimush," which means practical experience in Hebrew, underscores the idea that adaptation is essential for personal and societal resilience. It reflects the notion that adaptation is a means of thriving in a dynamic world.

Adaptation is not merely about survival; it encompasses a broader commitment to growth, learning, and flexibility. It's about recognizing that adaptation is not a sign of weakness but a manifestation of strength. It's a testament to the human spirit's ability to overcome challenges.

One remarkable aspect of adaptation is its potential to empower individuals and communities to navigate adversity and uncertainty. Adaptation allows us to transform setbacks into opportunities, to learn from failures, and to emerge stronger. This aligns with the universal principle that adaptation is a source of resilience.

The story of Jewish diaspora communities throughout history exemplifies the art of adaptation. In the face of adversity, these communities have displayed remarkable resilience and adaptability. They have maintained their traditions while embracing new cultures and environments.

Adaptation also intersects with the principle of "Hishtadlus." Many Jewish individuals and organizations understand the importance of proactive efforts to adapt to changing circumstances. They recognize that adaptation is not merely a reaction to change but a proactive strategy for growth.

As we delve deeper into the art of adaptation, we'll explore the qualities of adaptable individuals, the psychology of resilience, and the role of adaptation in personal and financial success. We'll draw inspiration from individuals and organizations that have embraced the art of adaptation to thrive in a changing world.

This chapter serves as a reminder that adaptation is not a one-time event but an ongoing process. The art of adaptation encourages us to embrace change, to learn from experience, and to cultivate the resilience needed to face the challenges of the future. In the chapters that follow, we'll continue our exploration, recognizing that each aspect of financial wisdom, whether it's ethics, community, networking, investment, the mindset of abundance, the dance of risk and reward, the art of financial planning, the legacy of philanthropy, the art of financial education, the entrepreneurial spirit, the art of innovation, the legacy of wisdom, the art of adaptation, the power of resilience, or the art of legacy, contributes to our holistic understanding of wealth and prosperity.

CHAPTER 32: THE POWER OF RESILIENCE

In our exploration of financial wisdom and its connection to the principles often associated with the Jewish community, we now delve into the concept of resilience. This chapter celebrates the power of resilience, a universal trait that enables individuals and communities to overcome adversity and emerge stronger.

Resilience is not bound by cultural or religious boundaries; it is a fundamental quality of the human spirit. It reflects the capacity to endure hardships, adapt to change, and persevere in the face of challenges. Resilience is the cornerstone of personal and financial success.

Within the Jewish tradition, there is a deep appreciation for the power of resilience. The principle of "Azut De'liba," which means strength of heart in Hebrew, underscores the idea that resilience is an essential attribute. It reflects the notion that resilience is not just a reaction to difficulties but a proactive approach to life's ups and downs.

Resilience is not about avoiding failure or adversity; it's about bouncing back from setbacks, learning from experiences, and growing stronger. It's about recognizing that resilience is not a fixed trait but a skill that can be cultivated and developed.

One remarkable aspect of resilience is its potential to transform adversity into opportunities for growth. Resilient individuals and communities often emerge from challenges with newfound wisdom, strength, and a sense of purpose. This aligns with the universal principle that resilience is a source of growth and transformation.

The stories of resilience within Jewish history and culture serve as inspiring examples. From the challenges faced by Jewish diaspora communities to the stories of individuals who have overcome adversity, the power of resilience is evident. It is a testament to the human spirit's ability to thrive in the face of adversity.

Resilience also intersects with the principle of "Bitachon." Many Jewish individuals and organizations understand the importance of trust in the face of uncertainty. They recognize that resilience is not just about inner strength but also about having faith in the future.

As we delve deeper into the power of resilience, we'll explore the qualities of resilient individuals, the psychology of bouncing back, and the role of resilience in achieving financial and personal goals. We'll draw inspiration from individuals and organizations that have harnessed the power of resilience to overcome challenges and achieve success.

This chapter serves as a reminder that resilience is not a rare trait possessed by a select few; it is a quality that can be cultivated by anyone. The power of resilience encourages us to face adversity with courage, to embrace change with adaptability, and to emerge from challenges with newfound strength.

CHAPTER 33: THE ART OF LEGACY

In our journey through the wisdom of wealth and prosperity, we now turn our attention to the concept of legacy. This chapter explores the profound idea of leaving a lasting legacy and how it aligns with the principles often associated with the Jewish community.

Legacy is a concept that transcends cultural or religious boundaries; it is the idea of creating a positive impact that endures beyond one's lifetime. Legacy is not merely about accumulating wealth; it is about using one's resources, knowledge, and influence to make a meaningful difference in the world.

Within the Jewish tradition, there is a deep reverence for the art of legacy. The principle of "Tikun Olam," which means repairing the world in Hebrew, underscores the idea that individuals have a responsibility to contribute to the betterment of society. It reflects the notion that legacy is not a passive act but an active commitment to social and ethical progress.

Legacy is about more than financial bequests; it encompasses the transmission of values, traditions, and wisdom to future generations. It's about instilling a sense of purpose and responsibility in those who follow. Legacy is a way of ensuring that one's influence continues to shape the world, even in their absence.

One remarkable aspect of legacy is its ability to inspire and motivate. Individuals and communities that are mindful of their legacy are often driven by a sense of purpose and a desire to leave the world a better place. They understand that their actions today have far-reaching consequences for the future.

The stories of Jewish scholars, leaders, and philanthropists who have left enduring legacies are inspiring examples. From contributions to education, healthcare, and social justice to the preservation of cultural heritage, the art of legacy is evident in various aspects of Jewish history and culture.

Legacy also intersects with the principle of "L'dor V'dor," which means from generation to generation. It embodies the idea that knowledge, values, and traditions are passed down through the ages. Legacy is about ensuring that the wisdom of the past continues to guide the future.

As we delve deeper into the art of legacy, we'll explore the qualities of individuals who have left lasting legacies, the psychology of legacy-building, and the role of legacy in achieving a sense of fulfillment and meaning in life. We'll draw inspiration from those who have harnessed the power of legacy to make a positive impact on the world.

This chapter serves as a reminder that legacy is not reserved for the exceptionally wealthy or famous; it is a concept that can be embraced by anyone. The art of legacy encourages us to reflect on our values, to consider the impact of our actions, and to leave a positive imprint on the world.

In the chapters that follow, we'll continue our exploration, recognizing that each aspect of financial wisdom, whether it's ethics, community, networking, investment, the mindset of abundance, the dance of risk and reward, the art of financial planning, the legacy of philanthropy, the art of financial education, the entrepreneurial spirit, the art of innovation, the legacy of wisdom, the art of adaptation, the power of resilience, the art of legacy, or the art of legacy, contributes to our holistic understanding of wealth and prosperity.

CHAPTER 34: THE ART OF FINANCIAL EDUCATION

In our exploration of the path to financial success, we arrive at a crucial point: the importance of financial education. While the principles of accumulating wealth are vital, the ability to understand and manage one's finances is equally essential.

Financial education is a cornerstone of financial empowerment. It equips individuals with the knowledge and skills needed to make informed financial decisions, navigate the complexities of the financial world, and build a secure future. In this chapter, we delve into the significance of financial education and how it connects with the principles we've explored thus far.

The Jewish tradition places a strong emphasis on the value of education. This reverence for learning extends to all aspects of life, including financial matters. The pursuit of knowledge is seen as a means to improve one's life and contribute to the betterment of society.

Financial education begins with the basics—the understanding of income, expenses, and savings. It progresses to more advanced concepts such as budgeting, investing, and retirement planning. A well-rounded financial education empowers individuals to take control of their financial destinies.

One noteworthy aspect of financial education is its potential to break the cycle of financial hardship. By providing individuals with the tools to manage their finances effectively, it offers a path to financial stability and independence.

Within the Jewish community, there are various initiatives and organizations dedicated to promoting financial literacy. These efforts recognize that financial education is a powerful means to uplift individuals and communities alike.

One of the fundamental principles of financial education is the idea that it's an ongoing journey. The financial landscape is continually evolving, and individuals must adapt and stay informed. The willingness to seek knowledge and stay updated on financial trends is a trait shared by many successful individuals.

Financial education also intersects with ethical considerations. It encourages individuals to make choices that align with their values and contribute positively to society. The ethical dimension of financial education highlights the importance of responsible investing and philanthropy.

In today's digital age, access to financial education has become more widespread than ever. Online courses, books, podcasts, and seminars offer a wealth of resources for those seeking to expand their financial knowledge. Moreover, many educational institutions recognize the importance of including financial literacy in their curriculum.

As we navigate the terrain of financial education, we'll explore the significance of mentorship and guidance in the process. We'll examine the stories of individuals who have used their financial education to achieve remarkable success and make meaningful contributions to their communities.

CHAPTER 35: THE POWER OF RESILIENCE IN WEALTH-BUILDING

Wealth-building is a journey filled with peaks and valleys, successes, and setbacks. In this chapter, we delve into the indispensable quality that can make or break one's financial journey: resilience.

Resilience is often defined as the ability to bounce back from adversity, to adapt and thrive in the face of challenges. It's a quality that many successful individuals share, and it plays a significant role in the pursuit of wealth, both in the Jewish tradition and beyond.

The path to financial success is rarely a straight line. There will be times when investments don't yield the expected returns, businesses face unexpected hurdles, or economic downturns affect personal finances. In such moments, resilience becomes a valuable asset.

One of the fundamental teachings in the Jewish tradition is the importance of perseverance and resilience in the face of adversity. It's embodied in the concept of "Hakarat Hatov," which means recognizing the good even in difficult situations. This perspective encourages individuals to find strength and growth opportunities in challenges.

Resilience is not just about enduring adversity; it's also about learning from it. In the world of finance, setbacks can be valuable teachers. They offer insights into risk management, the need for diversification, and the importance of contingency planning. A resilient individual takes these lessons to heart and applies them to future endeavors.

Another aspect of resilience is emotional strength. The ability to manage stress, anxiety, and fear during financial challenges is crucial. It enables individuals to make rational decisions rather than succumbing to panic. Emotional resilience is cultivated through self-awareness, mindfulness, and often, the support of a strong community.

Within the Jewish community, resilience has been a guiding force throughout history. Jewish people have faced numerous hardships, including periods of persecution and forced migration. Yet, they've demonstrated remarkable resilience in preserving their culture, values, and, in many cases, their wealth.

Resilience extends beyond the individual level to the community and even the nation. The ability to rebound from economic crises, adapt to changing circumstances, and support one another is at the core of resilient communities. In times of hardship, the strength of these communities often becomes a source of hope and support.

The financial world is replete with stories of individuals who faced substantial losses or failures but went on to achieve great success. These stories are a testament to the power of resilience. They highlight that setbacks need not define one's financial journey but can serve as stepping stones to greater achievements.

In the modern era, resilience is not only a personal trait but also a quality that can be developed and nurtured. Techniques such as stress management, positive thinking, and seeking mentorship are ways to strengthen one's resilience.

As we navigate the complexities of wealth-building, let's remember that resilience is a quality that can turn adversity into opportunity. It's the sturdy bridge that connects our aspirations with our achievements. In the chapters ahead, we'll explore how resilience is intertwined with other principles of financial success and discover inspiring stories of individuals who exemplify this remarkable trait.

CHAPTER 36: THE ART OF STRATEGIC GIVING

In the pursuit of wealth and success, there's a principle deeply ingrained in the Jewish tradition that holds great significance: the practice of charitable giving, known as "Tzedakah." This chapter explores the art of strategic giving and its role in not only accumulating wealth but also in making a positive impact on the world.

Charitable giving isn't solely an act of kindness; it's also a strategic approach to wealth management. In Judaism, the concept of Tzedakah isn't just about giving to those in need; it's about doing so with wisdom and intention. It's about making a difference while also considering the long-term effects on your financial well-being.

One of the fundamental principles of Tzedakah is the belief in the interconnectedness of all people. It recognizes that we share responsibility for the welfare of our fellow human beings and that helping others ultimately benefits society as a whole. This interconnectedness aligns with a broader perspective in the world of finance: that wealth creation isn't a zero-sum game, and a thriving society benefits everyone.

Strategic giving involves thoughtful planning and consideration of where your contributions will have the most significant impact. It's about identifying causes and organizations that resonate with your values and goals. Just as one diversifies their investment portfolio, diversifying your charitable giving can be a strategic move. This approach ensures that your contributions support a range of causes, mitigating risk, and maximizing the potential for positive change.

Furthermore, it's essential to assess the effectiveness and efficiency of charitable organizations. In the same way, you'd scrutinize an investment opportunity, evaluating a charity's financial transparency, and the percentage of donations allocated to actual programs is crucial. This ensures that your giving is both meaningful and impactful.

Strategic giving can extend to creating lasting legacies through endowments and foundations. Many successful individuals have established charitable foundations to perpetuate their philanthropic missions beyond their lifetimes. This approach allows your wealth to continue making a difference for generations to come.

Within the Jewish tradition, there's a concept called "Ma'aser Kesafim," which means giving one-tenth of your income to charity. While this may seem like a significant commitment, it's a practice rooted in the belief that sharing a portion of your earnings with those in need not only fulfills a moral duty but also invites blessings into your life.

Strategic giving is a powerful tool for networking and building connections within your community and beyond. In the world of finance, these connections can lead to valuable opportunities, partnerships, and insights. Giving with sincerity and humility often opens doors and creates a network of goodwill.

Moreover, the act of giving can provide a profound sense of fulfillment and purpose beyond financial success. It reminds us of the values that guide our journey and helps maintain perspective amidst the pursuit of wealth.

CHAPTER 37: NAVIGATING THE WATERS OF RISK AND REWARD

In the intricate dance of wealth creation, risk and reward are constant companions. This chapter delves into the dynamic relationship between risk and reward, exploring how successful individuals, including those from the Jewish tradition, have mastered the art of navigating these treacherous waters.

Risk is the daring venture into the unknown, the leap of faith, and the acknowledgment that the path to prosperity is fraught with uncertainties. In the world of finance, risk comes in many forms, from market volatility to economic downturns, and from entrepreneurial ventures to investment choices.

However, risk is not merely an obstacle but a stepping stone to success. Jewish culture and tradition have a profound understanding of the concept of risk-taking. The story of Jewish entrepreneurship and innovation is replete with examples of individuals who ventured into uncharted territory, often with little more than a vision and determination.

One such example is the Jewish immigrant experience in the United States during the late 19th and early 20th centuries. Fleeing persecution and seeking economic opportunity, many Jewish immigrants arrived on American shores with little more than the clothes on their backs. They faced language barriers, discrimination, and economic hardship. Yet, through their perseverance and willingness to take calculated risks, they established successful businesses and played a significant role in shaping the American economy.

Risk, when managed wisely, can yield significant rewards. It's about striking a balance between boldness and caution, harnessing your instincts and intellect, and making informed decisions. In the world of investments, diversification is a risk mitigation strategy that seeks to spread investments across different asset classes, reducing the impact of poor performance in any one area.

Additionally, successful individuals often embrace the concept of "measured risk." This means carefully assessing the potential rewards against the potential losses and making informed choices based on data, analysis, and market conditions. The ability to assess risk and make informed decisions is a skill that can be honed through education and experience.

The Jewish tradition also emphasizes the importance of seeking advice and guidance from trusted mentors and advisors. Building a network of knowledgeable individuals who can provide insights and perspective can be invaluable in making sound financial decisions. This practice aligns with the broader concept of networking, which we discussed in a previous chapter.

Understanding your risk tolerance is a crucial aspect of wealth management. It involves a deep self-assessment of your willingness and capacity to endure fluctuations in the pursuit of long-term financial goals. Risk tolerance can vary greatly among individuals, and it's essential to align your investment strategy with your personal comfort level.

Furthermore, risk is not confined to financial matters alone. It extends to other aspects of life, including career choices and entrepreneurship. The Jewish tradition encourages individuals to pursue meaningful work and ventures that align with their values and passions, even if they entail some level of risk. This alignment of personal values and financial endeavors can lead to a more fulfilling and purpose-driven life.

CHAPTER 38: THE POWER OF RESILIENCE: LESSONS FROM JEWISH HISTORY

In the tapestry of human history, resilience stands as a testament to the indomitable human spirit. It's the ability to endure adversity, adapt to change, and emerge stronger from the crucible of life's challenges. Throughout history, the Jewish community has exemplified resilience in the face of immense hardships, offering valuable lessons for navigating the turbulent waters of life.

Resilience is not a trait exclusive to any one group, but Jewish history provides us with a profound example of how resilience can shape the destiny of a community. The Jewish people have faced persecution, displacement, and discrimination for centuries, yet they have persisted, thrived, and contributed immeasurably to the world.

One remarkable facet of Jewish resilience is the preservation of cultural identity and traditions. Despite the diaspora and dispersion across the globe, Jewish communities have maintained a strong connection to their heritage. The commitment to passing down traditions, stories, and values from one generation to the next has been a source of strength and continuity.

Resilience often emerges from a deep sense of community and mutual support. In Jewish tradition, the concept of "Kehillah" (community) is of paramount importance. Communities provide a safety net, a sense of belonging, and a shared purpose. They are a source of emotional and practical support during challenging times.

The lesson here is that building strong relationships and connections can be a pillar of resilience. In our interconnected world, nurturing relationships with family, friends, mentors, and colleagues can provide invaluable support when facing adversity. These bonds can serve as a safety net, offering guidance, encouragement, and a sense of belonging.

Another crucial aspect of resilience is adaptability. Throughout their history, Jewish communities have demonstrated an ability to adapt to new environments and circumstances. This adaptability has enabled them to thrive in diverse cultural, economic, and political landscapes.

In today's fast-paced world, adaptability remains a key asset. Whether in the face of career changes, technological disruptions, or personal setbacks, the capacity to pivot, learn, and grow is essential. Adaptability often involves embracing change as an opportunity for growth rather than a setback.

Moreover, resilience is intertwined with the pursuit of knowledge and education. The Jewish tradition places a high value on learning, symbolized by the Talmud and Torah. This emphasis on education has not only preserved cultural and religious traditions but has also empowered individuals to excel in various fields.

In contemporary society, the pursuit of knowledge remains a powerful driver of success. Lifelong learning, whether through formal education or self-directed study, equips individuals with the skills and insights needed to navigate an ever-changing world.

Lastly, resilience is about maintaining hope, even in the darkest of times. The Jewish concept of "Tikvah" (hope) underscores the importance of maintaining optimism and faith in the future. Hope can be a source of motivation and strength, enabling individuals to persevere through adversity.

As we move forward in this book's exploration of wealth and success, remember that resilience is not just a quality; it's a mindset. It's a perspective that views challenges as opportunities, setbacks as stepping stones, and adversity as a test of character. Resilience is the force that propels individuals to overcome obstacles and achieve remarkable feats.

CHAPTER 39: INNOVATION AND THE WEALTH OF IDEAS

In the ever-evolving landscape of wealth and success, one factor consistently emerges as a driving force: innovation. The ability to generate fresh ideas, devise creative solutions, and adapt to changing circumstances is the lifeblood of prosperity. In this chapter, we will explore the profound impact of innovation on the journey to wealth and success.

Innovation is often associated with groundbreaking inventions and technological marvels, but its scope extends far beyond that. It encompasses a mindset that values curiosity, problem-solving, and forward thinking. Those who harness the power of innovation are not limited to a specific field or industry; they are individuals who approach challenges with a willingness to explore new avenues.

Consider the story of Thomas Edison, one of history's most prolific inventors. Edison's innovations spanned multiple industries, from the invention of the phonograph to the creation of the modern electric light bulb. His success was not solely attributed to his brilliance but also to his relentless pursuit of solutions. Edison famously stated, "I have not failed. I've just found 10,000 ways that won't work." This resilience and adaptability were hallmarks of his innovative spirit.

In the business world, innovation is a cornerstone of success. Companies that fail to adapt and innovate often find themselves overshadowed by competitors. The story of Apple Inc. under the leadership of Steve Jobs exemplifies this principle. Apple's success was not merely the result of producing superior products but also of redefining entire industries through innovation. The iPod, iPhone, and iPad revolutionized the way we interact with technology and media.

But innovation is not limited to individuals or corporations. Communities and societies that embrace innovation thrive as well. Consider the city of Singapore, which has transformed itself from a small trading post to a global financial hub. Singapore's success story is attributed to its leaders' visionary thinking, innovation in urban planning, and a commitment to excellence in education and healthcare.

Innovative thinking also plays a pivotal role in addressing global challenges. The advent of the Green Revolution in agriculture, led by figures like Norman Borlaug, saved millions from hunger. Innovations in renewable energy, medical research, and environmental conservation hold the promise of a brighter future for humanity.

While innovation often involves technological advancements, it also includes creative approaches to social, economic, and environmental issues. Innovators like Muhammad Yunus, who pioneered microfinance to alleviate poverty, remind us that innovative thinking can lead to profound social change.

In our interconnected world, innovation knows no borders. Collaborative innovation, facilitated by global communication and cooperation, has the potential to address complex global challenges. The development of vaccines in record time during the COVID-19 pandemic is a testament to the power of collaborative innovation.

As we navigate the path to wealth and success, we must cultivate an innovative mindset. This involves nurturing curiosity, embracing change, and viewing challenges as opportunities for growth. It means seeking novel solutions to problems and being open to feedback and collaboration.

CHAPTER 40: THE POWER OF RESILIENCE

Resilience – a trait that transcends cultures, transcends time, and transcends circumstances. It's a quality that often separates those who achieve lasting success from those who falter in the face of adversity. In this chapter, we delve into the profound influence of resilience on the path to wealth and success.

The journey to success is rarely a smooth one. It's marked by setbacks, failures, and unforeseen challenges. But what distinguishes those who ultimately succeed is their ability to bounce back, to adapt, and to persevere.

Let's take a journey through history and explore the lives of individuals who epitomized resilience.

Winston Churchill: Known for his leadership during World War II, Churchill's path to greatness was far from easy. He faced political setbacks, personal failures, and even depression. Yet, his unwavering determination and resilience in the face of immense pressure made him one of the 20th century's most iconic leaders.

Oprah Winfrey: Oprah's story is one of remarkable resilience. She rose from a challenging upbringing marked by poverty and abuse to become one of the most influential media moguls in the world. Her ability to overcome obstacles and turn adversity into opportunities is a testament to her resilience.

Nelson Mandela: Imprisoned for 27 years for his fight against apartheid, Mandela's resilience in the face of injustice is legendary. He emerged from prison with an unwavering commitment to reconciliation, eventually becoming South Africa's first black president and a global symbol of peace and resilience.

Resilience isn't limited to the famous; it's a quality found in countless individuals who've achieved success in various fields. Entrepreneurs who faced bankruptcy before building successful empires, athletes who overcame career-threatening injuries, and scientists who persisted through countless failures – they all share a common thread of resilience.

So, what exactly is resilience, and how can it be cultivated?

At its core, resilience is the ability to adapt and thrive in the face of adversity. It involves emotional strength, mental fortitude, and a growth mindset. Resilient individuals don't view failure as the end but as a stepping stone toward success. They embrace challenges as opportunities to learn and grow.

Resilience is built upon several key pillars:

Emotional Intelligence: Resilient individuals understand and manage their emotions effectively. They're not overwhelmed by setbacks but use their emotional awareness to find constructive ways forward.

Optimism: A positive outlook can be a powerful driver of resilience. Optimistic individuals are more likely to see setbacks as temporary and solvable, motivating them to persevere.

Adaptability: Resilience involves the ability to adapt to changing circumstances. This means being open to new ideas, strategies, and approaches when the old ones aren't working.

Social Support: Resilience is often nurtured by strong social networks. Having people who believe in you, support you, and provide encouragement can make a world of difference when facing challenges.

Self-Compassion: Resilient individuals are kind to themselves, even in the face of failure. They don't engage in self-criticism but rather practice self-compassion, acknowledging that everyone faces setbacks.

Purpose: A clear sense of purpose can provide a powerful anchor during difficult times. When you have a compelling "why," it becomes easier to weather the storms on your path.

Cultivating resilience is an ongoing process. It involves developing these pillars through self-awareness, practice, and continuous growth. Resilience isn't about avoiding failure or adversity – it's about embracing them as part of the journey and using them as stepping stones toward success.

As we continue our exploration of the elements that shape wealth and success, remember that resilience is your shield against life's uncertainties. It's your capacity to bounce back, learn from setbacks, and forge ahead, no matter the challenges that come your way.

CHAPTER 41: THE ART OF EFFECTIVE COMMUNICATION

Effective communication is a superpower. It's a skill that can open doors, build bridges, and bring about profound transformations in your personal and professional life. In this chapter, we'll dive deep into the art of communication and how it influences your journey towards success.

Think about the most successful people you know – whether they're business leaders, politicians, or artists. What sets them apart? Undoubtedly, one of the defining factors is their ability to communicate effectively. They can convey their ideas, inspire others, and navigate complex situations with finesse.

Let's explore the facets of effective communication and how they can serve as a catalyst on your path to success.

1. Listening as the Foundation: Effective communication begins with listening. Truly listening, not just hearing. It's about paying full attention to what others are saying, understanding their perspectives, and valuing their input. When you listen actively, you create an atmosphere of trust and respect.

2. Clear and Concise Expression: Clarity is key. Whether you're giving a presentation, negotiating a deal, or simply having a conversation, the ability to express your ideas clearly and concisely is paramount. Complex jargon and convoluted sentences can lead to confusion. Simplicity in communication is often more persuasive.

3. Non-Verbal Communication: Words are only part of the

equation. Your body language, facial expressions, and tone of voice all contribute to your message. They can convey confidence or uncertainty, trustworthiness or suspicion. Being aware of your non-verbal cues and using them intentionally can greatly enhance your communication skills.

4. Empathy and Emotional Intelligence: Understanding the emotions of others is a cornerstone of effective communication. Empathy allows you to connect on a deeper level, to acknowledge and validate feelings, and to respond with sensitivity. Emotional intelligence helps you manage your own emotions and navigate emotionally charged situations.

5. Adaptability: Effective communicators are adaptable. They tailor their communication style to their audience, whether it's a team of employees, a group of investors, or a casual conversation with a friend. Being able to adjust your approach and language ensures your message resonates with the people you're addressing.

6. Constructive Feedback: Giving and receiving feedback is an essential part of communication. Constructive feedback can help individuals and organizations grow and improve. Learning to provide feedback in a way that is specific, actionable, and respectful is a skill worth honing.

7. Storytelling: Humans are hardwired for stories. Effective communicators often use storytelling to convey their message. Stories engage emotions, make information memorable, and create a compelling narrative that captures attention.

8. Conflict Resolution: Conflict is a natural part of human interactions, especially in high-stakes environments. Effective communicators are adept at resolving conflicts constructively. They can find common ground, mediate disputes, and maintain relationships even in challenging situations.

9. Authenticity: Authenticity breeds trust. When you communicate authentically, you're honest, transparent, and true to yourself. People are drawn to authenticity because it signals integrity and sincerity.

10. Continuous Improvement: Communication is a lifelong

journey. There's always room for improvement. Seek feedback, practice active listening, read about communication strategies, and learn from great communicators around you.

CHAPTER 42: THE POWER OF RESILIENCE: THRIVING THROUGH LIFE'S CHALLENGES

Life, in all its beauty, can sometimes be a rollercoaster of challenges. At some point, we all face setbacks, adversity, and moments when it feels like the world is conspiring against us. It's during these times that the power of resilience truly shines.

Resilience is the capacity to bounce back from adversity, to adapt to change, and to keep going despite life's curveballs. It's not a fixed trait; it's a skill that can be developed and honed over time. In this chapter, we'll explore resilience and how it can be your ally on the journey to success.

Understanding Resilience

Resilience isn't about being impervious to hardship; it's about how you respond to it. It's not just about enduring pain, but also about growing from it. Resilient individuals tend to have several characteristics in common:

Optimism: They maintain a positive outlook even in difficult situations. They see setbacks as temporary and believe in their ability to overcome them.

Problem-Solving Skills: Resilient people are resourceful. They can assess challenges objectively, identify potential solutions, and take action.

Social Support: Having a network of friends, family, or colleagues who offer emotional support is crucial for resilience. Knowing you're not alone can provide strength.

Self-Compassion: Resilient individuals practice self-compassion, treating themselves with the same kindness and understanding they would offer to a friend.

Adaptability: They are flexible and can adjust their goals or plans when necessary. They recognize that life rarely goes according to a linear path.

Building Resilience

Resilience is a muscle that can be strengthened. Here are some strategies to develop your resilience:

Cultivate a Growth Mindset: Embrace challenges as opportunities for growth. Instead of seeing failures as setbacks, view them as stepping stones toward success.

Maintain Perspective: Keep hardships in perspective. Ask yourself if the situation will matter in the grand scheme of your life. Often, we blow things out of proportion.

Practice Self-Care: Taking care of your physical and mental health is essential. Eat well, exercise, get enough sleep, and engage in activities that bring you joy.

Set Realistic Goals: While ambition is commendable, setting achievable goals can help you avoid feeling overwhelmed. Break big tasks into smaller, manageable steps.

Seek Support: Don't hesitate to lean on your support network. Sharing your challenges and feelings with others can provide valuable insights and comfort.

Learn from Adversity: After a challenging experience, reflect on what you've learned and how you've grown. This perspective can help you face future obstacles with confidence.

Resilience and Success

Success isn't a destination; it's a journey marked by both triumphs and setbacks. Resilience is your companion on this journey, helping you weather storms, adapt to change, and emerge stronger. It's what allows you to persist when others might give up.

Consider the stories of successful individuals who faced tremendous adversity: Oprah Winfrey, who overcame a difficult childhood to become a media mogul; Elon Musk, who faced multiple failures before achieving SpaceX and Tesla; J.K. Rowling, who was rejected by numerous publishers before creating the Harry Potter series.

Their stories illustrate the transformative power of resilience. Each setback they encountered became a stepping stone to their ultimate success. Their stories are not isolated incidents but part of a broader narrative that connects the chapters of this book.

CHAPTER 43: THE ART OF EFFECTIVE COMMUNICATION

Communication is the lifeblood of human interaction. It's the bridge that connects us, allowing us to convey thoughts, feelings, and ideas. But effective communication is an art, one that can transform personal and professional relationships, ensuring they thrive rather than stagnate.

In this chapter, we'll explore the nuances of effective communication, providing you with valuable insights and strategies to enhance this critical skill.

The Power of Listening

At the heart of effective communication lies the art of listening. Truly listening, not just waiting for your turn to speak, is a profound skill that can transform your interactions. When you actively listen, you convey respect and empathy, which are essential for building trust and rapport.

Here are some principles of active listening:

Give Your Full Attention: When someone is speaking to you, put away distractions. Make eye contact, nod, or use other non-verbal cues to show that you're engaged.

Avoid Interrupting: Let the speaker finish their thoughts before you respond. Interruptions can disrupt the flow of conversation and convey disrespect.

Ask Open-Ended Questions: Encourage the speaker to share more by asking questions that can't be answered with a simple "yes" or "no." For example, instead of asking, "Did you have a good weekend?" ask, "What did you do over the weekend?"

Reflect and Clarify: After the speaker has shared, reflect back what you've heard to ensure you understood correctly. You can say something like, "So, if I understand correctly, you're saying..."

The Art of Empathy

Empathy is the ability to understand and share the feelings of another. It's a fundamental component of effective communication. When you express empathy, you create a safe space for others to open up and share their thoughts and emotions.

Empathetic communication involves:

Acknowledging Feelings: If someone expresses sadness, frustration, or joy, acknowledge their emotions. For example, "I can see that this situation has been really tough for you."

Avoiding Judgment: Refrain from passing judgment or offering unsolicited advice. Sometimes, people simply need someone to listen and empathize.

Validating Emotions: Let the person know that their feelings are valid. You can say, "It's completely understandable that you would feel this way."

Clarity and Conciseness

Effective communication also involves clarity and conciseness. Being clear in your message ensures that your intended meaning is received accurately. Avoid jargon or complex language that might confuse your audience.

Consider your audience's needs and tailor your message accordingly. For example, if you're explaining a complex concept to someone unfamiliar with the subject, use simple language and provide relatable examples.

Non-Verbal Communication

Non-verbal cues play a significant role in communication. These cues include body language, facial expressions, tone of voice, and even the spacing between words. In fact, research suggests that non-verbal communication can convey more meaning than words themselves.

Be mindful of your non-verbal cues, as they can either enhance or undermine your message. Maintain eye contact, use an open posture, and modulate your tone of voice to match the content of your message.

Feedback and Adaptation

Effective communication is a dynamic process that requires feedback and adaptation. Pay attention to how your message is received. If you notice confusion or misinterpretation, be willing to clarify and rephrase. Communication is a two-way street, and ensuring that your message is understood is your responsibility as a communicator.

The Connection to Resilience

Effective communication is intrinsically linked to resilience. When faced with challenges, the ability to express your thoughts and feelings clearly can help you seek support and find solutions. Moreover, empathetic communication allows you to connect with others who may be going through similar hardships.

CHAPTER 44: THE JOURNEY OF PERSONAL GROWTH

In the intricate tapestry of human existence, one thread remains constant: the pursuit of personal growth and self-improvement. As we navigate the labyrinthine pathways of life, we often find ourselves striving for a better version of who we are. This chapter explores the fascinating journey of personal growth, a continuous process that enriches our lives in myriad ways.

Embracing Change

At its core, personal growth is about embracing change. Change, though often daunting, is the catalyst for progress. It's the chisel that sculpts the masterpiece of your life. Change can manifest in various forms, from learning a new skill to adopting healthier habits, or even shifting your mindset.

Consider the individual who decides to learn a musical instrument in their adult years. This seemingly simple act embodies personal growth. It requires dedication, patience, and resilience. The journey involves challenges, like deciphering sheet music or mastering finger placements. Yet, with persistence, the person progresses, and the sense of accomplishment fuels their personal growth.

The Role of Adversity

Adversity, while unwelcome, plays a significant role in personal growth. Life's difficulties often serve as the crucible where our character is tested and refined. These trials, whether in the form of setbacks, losses, or heartaches, have the power to transform us.

Take, for example, the story of a young entrepreneur whose first business venture failed spectacularly. Crushed by financial losses and beset by self-doubt, they could have given up. Instead, they chose to view this setback as an opportunity for growth. They analyzed their mistakes, honed their skills, and embarked on a new entrepreneurial journey. The lessons learned from their initial failure were the stepping stones to later success.

Learning from Others

Personal growth isn't a solitary endeavor. Learning from others can accelerate your journey. Consider the wisdom of mentors and the insights gained from sharing experiences with peers. By seeking guidance and advice, you tap into a collective pool of knowledge.

Furthermore, reading biographies and autobiographies of accomplished individuals can provide valuable lessons. These accounts offer a glimpse into the challenges, triumphs, and personal growth of those who have walked diverse paths. Whether it's the life story of a renowned scientist, an influential leader, or a celebrated artist, you can draw inspiration from their journeys.

The Mind-Body Connection

Another crucial aspect of personal growth is the mind-body connection. Physical well-being has a profound impact on your mental state, and vice versa. Engaging in regular exercise, maintaining a balanced diet, and practicing mindfulness techniques can all contribute to holistic personal growth.

Exercise, for instance, releases endorphins, often referred to as "feel-good" hormones. These chemicals boost mood and reduce stress, ultimately fostering a positive mental state. Similarly, a balanced diet rich in nutrients fuels cognitive function and supports emotional well-being.

Finding Purpose

The journey of personal growth often intersects with the search for purpose. As you grow and evolve, your understanding of your life's purpose may shift. What once seemed important may give way to new aspirations and passions.

Finding purpose is a deeply individual quest. Some discover it through their careers, others through creative pursuits, and still, others through acts of service and philanthropy. The key is to remain open to the evolving nature of your purpose and to embrace it when it reveals itself.

The Connection to Resilience

Personal growth and resilience are intertwined. The lessons learned through personal growth—such as adaptability, perseverance, and self-awareness—are the very qualities that fortify your resilience. When adversity strikes, a growth-oriented mindset empowers you to navigate challenges with grace and determination.

As we continue our journey through the chapters of this book, you'll encounter stories of individuals whose paths of personal growth intersect with their experiences of resilience. These stories will illuminate the dynamic interplay between self-improvement and the ability to overcome life's obstacles.

CHAPTER 45: THE POWER OF RESILIENCE: STORIES THAT INSPIRE

In the intricate tapestry of human existence, one thread shines brightly: resilience. It's the quality that allows individuals to withstand life's storms, to bend but not break in the face of adversity. Resilience is like a hidden superpower that resides within us all, waiting to be summoned when needed most. This chapter explores the incredible power of resilience through stories that inspire and illuminate the human capacity to triumph over challenges.

The Phoenix Rises: Rebuilding After Loss

Consider the story of Sarah, a mother who faced the unimaginable loss of her home in a devastating fire. Everything she had worked for, her cherished possessions, and even the tangible memories of her family were reduced to ashes. In the aftermath, it would have been easy for despair to consume her.

But Sarah was determined to rise from the ashes, much like the mythical phoenix. She found strength in the support of her community, the love of her family, and her own indomitable spirit. Instead of succumbing to grief, she channeled her energy into rebuilding her life. The experience, while incredibly challenging, ultimately revealed her inner resilience. Sarah's story teaches us that resilience can emerge even in the darkest of times, showing us the depth of our own inner strength.

The Marathon of Life: Overcoming Chronic Illness

Resilience isn't solely about bouncing back from singular traumatic events; it's also about endurance in the face of chronic challenges. Consider the story of Alex, a young man diagnosed with a debilitating chronic illness that threatened to hijack his dreams and aspirations.

Living with chronic illness often feels like running a marathon with no finish line in sight. But Alex didn't let his diagnosis define him. Instead, he embarked on a journey of self-discovery, seeking treatments, adapting his lifestyle, and building a support network. It wasn't easy, but he refused to surrender to despair. Over time, Alex not only managed his condition but also found a new purpose—advocating for others facing similar struggles. His resilience turned his personal battle into a source of inspiration for countless individuals who saw in him the embodiment of hope.

From Pain to Purpose: Transforming Trauma into Advocacy

Sometimes, resilience emerges from the crucible of trauma. Consider the story of Maya, who endured a traumatic event that left deep emotional scars. Instead of succumbing to the shadows of her past, Maya transformed her pain into purpose.

Maya's journey of resilience led her to become an advocate for trauma survivors. Through counseling, education, and outreach, she helped others navigate the difficult path to healing. Her story illustrates how resilience can become a beacon, guiding us towards meaningful contributions to the world, even after enduring profound hardship.

The Dance of Adaptation: Thriving in a Changing World

Resilience also thrives in the realm of adaptation. Think of James, a professional in an industry disrupted by rapid technological advances. His well-established career became obsolete seemingly overnight, leaving him at a crossroads.

Instead of clinging to the past, James embraced change with open arms. He saw an opportunity for reinvention, reskilling, and venturing into a new field. His adaptability, the cornerstone of resilience, allowed him to carve a fresh path filled with exciting opportunities.

Resilience Across Generations: A Family's Legacy

The stories of resilience aren't limited to individuals; they resonate through generations. Imagine a family that faced adversity during challenging times, whether due to economic downturns, health crises, or personal struggles. Each generation drew inspiration from the resilience of their forebears, passing down the legacy of strength and perseverance.

These intergenerational stories serve as a testament to the enduring power of resilience. They remind us that the ability to overcome obstacles often runs in our veins, weaving through our family histories like a cherished heirloom.

The Threads of Resilience

As we explore these stories of resilience, we uncover the common threads that bind them together—courage, determination, adaptability, and unwavering hope. Resilience isn't a fixed trait; it's a dynamic quality that can be cultivated and strengthened. These narratives demonstrate that resilience isn't the absence of adversity; it's the triumph over it.

CHAPTER 46: THE TRANSFORMATIVE POWER OF MINDFULNESS

In the hustle and bustle of modern life, there's a persistent undercurrent of restlessness. We rush from one task to the next, distracted by a constant stream of information, and often find ourselves living on autopilot. It's in these moments of mindless living that we miss the richness of life itself. In this chapter, we'll explore the transformative power of mindfulness—a practice that brings us back to the present moment, enabling us to experience life more fully.

The Elixir of Presence

Mindfulness is the art of being fully present, without judgment, in the current moment. It's a state of heightened awareness that allows us to observe our thoughts, feelings, and sensations without getting entangled in them. This practice, often associated with meditation, has roots in ancient traditions like Buddhism but has found a place in our modern, fast-paced world.

Imagine a typical morning: You wake up to the blaring sound of an alarm clock, immediately jump out of bed, and rush through your morning routine. You're thinking about your to-do list, the tasks at work, and the traffic you'll encounter on your commute. Breakfast is a hurried affair, with your mind already racing ahead. In this scenario, the morning becomes a blur, and you've missed the opportunity to fully experience it.

Now, imagine a different morning. You wake up to the same alarm, but instead of leaping out of bed, you take a moment to notice the sensation of your body waking up. You feel the warmth of the sunlight streaming through your window. As you eat your breakfast, you savor each bite, truly tasting the flavors. Your mind is fully engaged in the act of eating, not drifting to other concerns. This is mindfulness in action.

The Power of Presence

Why does mindfulness matter, you might ask? The benefits are manifold and backed by scientific research. Here are a few ways in which mindfulness can transform your life:

Reducing Stress: Mindfulness helps break the cycle of stress by allowing you to respond to life's challenges with greater calm and clarity. By focusing on the present moment, you can step out of the whirlwind of anxiety that often accompanies stressful situations.

Enhancing Emotional Regulation: Mindfulness provides a toolkit for managing your emotions. It allows you to observe your feelings without immediately reacting to them. This emotional intelligence can lead to healthier relationships and better decision-making.

Improving Concentration: In a world filled with distractions, the ability to concentrate is a valuable skill. Mindfulness enhances your attention span by training your mind to stay on a chosen focal point, whether it's your breath, bodily sensations, or the sounds around you.

Boosting Creativity: When you're fully present, you open the door to creativity. You're more likely to make novel connections and see problems from fresh perspectives.

Enhancing Physical Health: Mindfulness has been linked to various physical health benefits, including lower blood pressure, improved sleep, and a strengthened immune system. When you're less stressed and more attuned to your body, it naturally responds with improved well-being.

Incorporating Mindfulness into Your Life

The practice of mindfulness doesn't require a dramatic overhaul of your daily routine. You can begin by integrating small mindful moments into your day:

Mindful Breathing: Take a few minutes each day to focus on your breath. Observe its natural rhythm, and when your mind wanders (as it inevitably will), gently guide your attention back to your breath.

Mindful Eating: During meals, put away distractions like phones or screens. Savor each bite, paying attention to the flavors, textures, and the act of chewing.

Mindful Walking: As you walk, notice the sensation of each step—the way your feet touch the ground, the movement of your body, and the sounds around you.

Mindful Pauses: Throughout your day, pause for a few moments to simply be. Take in your surroundings, your feelings, and your thoughts without judgment.

Mindful Listening: When in conversation with others, truly listen. Instead of formulating your response while they speak, give them your full attention.

The Journey Continues

Mindfulness is a journey, not a destination. As you continue your exploration of this practice, you'll likely encounter moments of resistance or frustration. That's perfectly normal. The essence of mindfulness is to observe these moments without judgment and gently guide yourself back to the present.

CHAPTER 47: THE ART OF STORYTELLING: CRAFTING YOUR NARRATIVE

Stories are the lifeblood of human communication. From the ancient myths passed down through generations to the latest bestselling novels, stories shape our understanding of the world and connect us to one another. In this chapter, we'll explore the art of storytelling and how you can craft your narrative to captivate, inspire, and communicate effectively.

The Power of Storytelling

Stories are universal. They transcend borders, languages, and cultures. Since the dawn of humanity, we've used stories to make sense of our experiences, share knowledge, and communicate our deepest emotions. Here are a few reasons why storytelling is such a potent tool:

Engagement: Stories grab our attention and hold it. Whether it's a gripping mystery or a heartwarming tale, a well-told story keeps us hooked from beginning to end.

Emotion: Stories evoke emotions. They can make us laugh, cry, feel anger, or experience joy. When you want to convey a message that resonates, embedding it in a story is often the most effective approach.

Memorability: We remember stories much better than we remember dry facts or data. That's why anecdotes and narratives are commonly used in education and marketing.

Connection: Stories create connections between people. When you share a personal story, others can relate to your experiences, fostering empathy and understanding.

Persuasion: If you want to convince someone of your point of view, a compelling story can be more persuasive than a list of arguments.

Crafting Your Narrative

Now, let's delve into the process of crafting your narrative. Whether you're writing a memoir, giving a presentation, or even just chatting with friends, these principles of storytelling can help you communicate effectively:

Know Your Audience: Tailor your story to your audience. Consider their interests, values, and what they're looking to gain from your narrative.

Structure Matters: Most stories have a beginning, middle, and end. The beginning sets the stage, the middle builds tension, and the end resolves it. Don't forget to include these elements in your storytelling.

Character Development: If your story involves characters (which it often should), spend time developing them. What are their motivations, flaws, and growth throughout the narrative?

Conflict and Resolution: Every good story has conflict, and it's through overcoming this conflict that characters grow. What obstacles do your characters face, and how do they resolve them?

Emotionally Resonant Themes: Think about the emotional themes you want to convey. Is your story about love, resilience, or the pursuit of knowledge? Weave these themes into your narrative.

Show, Don't Tell: Instead of explicitly stating how characters feel or what's happening, show it through actions, dialogue, and sensory details. Let your audience infer meaning.

Use Vivid Descriptions: Engage the senses with descriptive language. Help your audience see, hear, taste, smell, and touch the world you're creating.

Create Tension: Tension keeps your audience engaged. Pose questions, create mysteries, or introduce conflicts that keep people guessing.

Personal Connection: If you're sharing a personal story, be vulnerable. Share your thoughts, feelings, and experiences authentically. This builds trust and connection.

Practice, Practice, Practice: Whether you're telling a story verbally or in writing, practice is essential. Refine your narrative, seeking feedback if possible.

Storytelling Across Mediums

Storytelling isn't limited to the written word or spoken tales around a campfire. In today's digital age, storytelling can take many forms:

Written Stories: Novels, short stories, essays, and articles are the traditional written mediums for storytelling.

Visual Stories: Photography and filmmaking allow you to tell stories through visuals. The composition, colors, and framing of an image can convey powerful narratives.

Digital Storytelling: In the age of the internet, blogs, podcasts, and social media are platforms for sharing stories. With multimedia content, you can engage a diverse audience.

Interactive Stories: Video games and choose-your-own-adventure narratives offer interactive storytelling experiences, allowing players to shape the plot.

Oral Storytelling: From TED Talks to casual conversations, spoken storytelling is a potent way to engage and persuade.

Your Story Matters

Remember that your story, no matter how ordinary or extraordinary, is worth sharing. Your experiences, insights, and emotions can inspire and connect with others. Whether you're crafting a story for personal fulfillment or to communicate a message, storytelling is an art that enriches our lives and brings us closer together.

CHAPTER 48: THE ART OF PUBLIC SPEAKING: CAPTIVATING YOUR AUDIENCE

Public speaking remains one of the most feared and yet essential skills in the professional world. Whether you're addressing a large crowd, leading a meeting, or simply chatting with a group of friends, your ability to speak effectively can make or break your message. In this chapter, we'll explore the art of public speaking and how you can captivate your audience, leaving a lasting impact.

The Fear of Public Speaking

Before we dive into the nuances of public speaking, let's address the elephant in the room: the fear of public speaking. This fear, known as glossophobia, affects a significant portion of the population. It often stems from the fear of judgment, failure, or embarrassment in front of others. While it's normal to feel nervous before speaking in public, these fears can be managed and even overcome with practice and preparation.

The Essence of Effective Public Speaking

Effective public speaking is about more than just delivering information. It's about engaging, inspiring, and connecting with your audience. Here are some key principles to keep in mind:

Know Your Audience: Just as in storytelling, understanding your audience is crucial. Tailor your message to their interests, needs, and expectations.

Clear Structure: Every speech should have a clear structure. Start with an attention-grabbing introduction, follow with your main points, and conclude with a memorable closing statement.

Engaging Content: Your content should be interesting, relevant, and valuable to your audience. Avoid jargon and complex language when unnecessary.

Visual Aids: Visual aids, such as slides, can enhance your presentation, but they should complement your speech, not replace it. Use visuals sparingly and ensure they're easy to understand.

Body Language: Your body language communicates as much as your words. Maintain eye contact, use gestures naturally, and stand confidently. Good posture exudes confidence.

Voice and Tone: Vary your tone, pitch, and pace to keep your audience engaged. Use pauses strategically to emphasize points or allow your audience to digest information.

Storytelling: Weaving stories into your speech can make it more relatable and memorable. Stories have the power to evoke emotions and create a connection.

Audience Interaction: Encourage interaction with your audience through questions, polls, or discussion points. This keeps them actively engaged.

Practice: Rehearse your speech multiple times. Familiarity with your content reduces anxiety and helps you speak more confidently.

Feedback: Seek feedback from trusted individuals. They can provide valuable insights and help you refine your speech.

Overcoming Fear and Anxiety

If you're one of the many people who feel anxious about public speaking, here are some strategies to help overcome this fear:

Preparation: The more you prepare, the more confident you'll feel. Know your content inside and out.

Visualization: Spend time visualizing a successful speech. Imagine yourself speaking confidently and your audience responding positively.

Breathing Techniques: Deep, controlled breathing can calm

nerves. Practice breathing exercises before and during your speech.

Small Steps: Start with smaller, less intimidating speaking engagements before tackling larger ones.

Positive Self-Talk: Replace negative thoughts with positive affirmations. Remind yourself of your strengths and past successes.

Support Network: Seek support from friends, family, or a professional coach who can help you work through your fears.

The Ongoing Journey

Public speaking is a skill that can always be improved. Even experienced speakers continually refine their techniques. So, whether you're just starting your public speaking journey or looking to enhance your existing skills, remember that practice and perseverance will lead to growth.

CHAPTER 49: THE POWER OF EMPATHY IN HUMAN CONNECTIONS

Empathy, the ability to understand and share the feelings of another, is a fundamental human trait that plays a pivotal role in our relationships, both personal and professional. In this chapter, we delve into the profound significance of empathy in our lives, exploring how it fosters understanding, builds connections, and fuels personal growth.

The Essence of Empathy

Empathy is not a simple emotion but a complex cognitive and emotional skill. It involves the capacity to perceive the emotions, thoughts, and perspectives of others while maintaining our own emotional boundaries. This unique blend of understanding and emotional resonance forms the bedrock of meaningful human connections.

Empathy in Personal Relationships

In our personal lives, empathy is the glue that binds us to friends, family, and loved ones. When we empathize, we demonstrate that we care, that we see and understand the experiences of others. Here are ways empathy enriches personal relationships:

Conflict Resolution: Empathy allows us to see disagreements from another's point of view. This understanding often paves the way for compromise and resolution.

Support: When someone is going through a tough time, our

empathetic presence can provide solace and strength. Sometimes, all we need to do is listen and understand.

Connection: Empathy deepens our connections with others. It creates trust and vulnerability, fostering intimacy in relationships.

Forgiveness: Empathy helps us understand why others act as they do. This insight can make forgiveness a more attainable goal.

Personal Growth: By understanding others' experiences and viewpoints, we expand our own perspective and enrich our personal growth journey.

Empathy in Professional Settings

The significance of empathy isn't limited to our personal lives. In the workplace, empathy plays a critical role in leadership, teamwork, and customer relations. Here's how it makes a difference:

Leadership: Empathetic leaders are more attuned to the needs and concerns of their team members. They can motivate, inspire, and create a positive work environment.

Teamwork: Teams that operate with empathy communicate better, resolve conflicts more effectively, and achieve higher levels of collaboration and productivity.

Customer Relations: In business, understanding the needs and pain points of customers is vital. Empathy allows organizations to create products and services that genuinely address customer needs.

Developing Empathy

While some individuals naturally possess a high degree of empathy, it's a skill that can be cultivated and improved over time. Here are some strategies to enhance your empathetic abilities:

Active Listening: Truly listening to others without judgment is the foundation of empathy. Practice active listening by giving your full attention and asking clarifying questions.

Perspective-Taking: Put yourself in someone else's shoes. Imagine how they feel and think in a given situation.

Cultivate Curiosity: Be genuinely interested in other people's stories and experiences. Ask open-ended questions that encourage them to share.

Practice Self-Reflection: Regularly reflect on your own emotions and experiences. This can increase your awareness and empathy toward others.

Read Widely: Literature, biographies, and memoirs can offer insights into the lives and emotions of people from diverse backgrounds.

Empathy in Action: Act on your empathetic feelings. Offer help, support, or a kind word when you sense someone is in need.

Empathy's Ripple Effect

The beauty of empathy is that it has a ripple effect. When you show empathy to someone, they are more likely to reciprocate, creating a cycle of understanding and compassion. This ripple extends to your broader community and, ultimately, contributes to a more empathetic society.

CHAPTER 50: THE ART OF RESILIENCE – THRIVING AMIDST LIFE'S CHALLENGES

We've journeyed through 49 chapters, exploring diverse aspects of the human experience, from the mysteries of the cosmos to the depths of empathy. Now, we stand on the threshold of the final chapter, a chapter that encapsulates the very essence of human existence – resilience.

The Unyielding Spirit of Resilience

Resilience is the remarkable ability of the human spirit to withstand adversity, adapt to change, and emerge stronger from life's most daunting challenges. It is, in essence, the cornerstone of our survival and progress as a species.

The Nature of Adversity

Life, as we have come to understand, is not without its trials and tribulations. Adversity comes in various forms – personal, societal, or natural. Whether it's a personal loss, a global crisis, or a natural disaster, adversity tests the mettle of individuals and communities alike.

The Components of Resilience

Resilience is not a binary trait; it is multifaceted, comprised of several components that collectively empower individuals to endure and grow in the face of adversity:

Emotional Resilience: The ability to manage emotions effectively, even during times of stress, is a core component of resilience.

Emotionally resilient individuals can acknowledge their feelings, express them constructively, and regain emotional equilibrium.

Cognitive Resilience: Cognitive resilience refers to the capacity to maintain mental agility in the face of challenges. It involves problem-solving, adaptability, and the ability to reframe negative situations with a positive outlook.

Social Resilience: Humans are inherently social creatures, and our connections with others are vital for resilience. Strong social support networks, empathy, and effective communication are crucial in helping us weather life's storms.

Physical Resilience: Physical health plays a significant role in resilience. A strong, well-nourished body is better equipped to handle stress and recover from setbacks. Exercise, a balanced diet, and adequate rest contribute to physical resilience.

The Power of Growth Through Adversity

Resilience isn't merely about enduring hardships; it's about learning and growing from them. Adversity has the remarkable capacity to be a catalyst for personal development:

Adaptive Skills: When faced with challenges, we often acquire new skills and knowledge that enable us to overcome similar obstacles in the future.

Enhanced Perspective: Adversity can offer a fresh perspective on life. It prompts us to reevaluate our priorities, leading to greater clarity about what truly matters.

Increased Empathy: Experiencing hardship can make us more empathetic toward others who are facing similar challenges. It fosters a sense of shared humanity.

Strength of Character: Resilience strengthens our character. It builds confidence, tenacity, and a sense of self-worth that helps us face future challenges with greater determination.

Cultivating Resilience

Resilience is not a static trait; it can be cultivated and nurtured throughout life. Here are some strategies to enhance your resilience:

Build a Support Network: Cultivate meaningful relationships with friends, family, and colleagues. Seek support when needed and offer support to others in return.

Practice Self-Care: Prioritize your physical and mental health. Exercise regularly, eat well, and engage in activities that bring you joy and relaxation.

Develop Problem-Solving Skills: Enhance your ability to analyze and solve problems. Approach challenges with a growth mindset, viewing them as opportunities for growth and learning.

Embrace Change: Life is constantly changing. Instead of resisting change, embrace it as an opportunity for personal development.

Maintain Perspective: When facing adversity, step back and assess the bigger picture. Sometimes, challenges are temporary setbacks on a longer journey.

The Human Spirit's Triumph

As we conclude our exploration of the human experience, we do so with the knowledge that resilience is our enduring legacy. Throughout history, humanity has faced countless trials and emerged stronger, demonstrating the indomitable spirit that characterizes our species.

In the grand tapestry of existence, each chapter reveals a facet of the intricate human experience. From the boundless universe to the depths of our souls, from the wonders of science to the mysteries of consciousness, and from the power of empathy to the art of resilience, our journey through these 50 chapters serves as a testament to the richness, complexity, and boundless potential of the human narrative.

As we close this book, remember that the story of humanity is ongoing, with each individual contributing their own unique chapter. The pages may turn, but the enduring essence of our humanity remains – the relentless pursuit of understanding, connection, and growth in the remarkable story of us.

www.ingramcontent.com/pod-product-compliance
Lightning Source LLC
Chambersburg PA
CBHW050315230526
45471CB00005B/2198